GOOD
HOUSEKEEPING
*Growing Food in
Your Greenhouse*

Other gardening books by Sheila Howarth

Gardening
Handbook of Easy Garden Plants
Good Housekeeping Vegetable Growing

GOOD HOUSEKEEPING
Growing Food in Your Greenhouse

by Sheila Howarth
illustrated by C R Evans

EBURY PRESS *London*

Published by Ebury Press
National Magazine House
72 Broadwick Street
London W1V 2BP

First impression 1979
Second impression 1979

ISBN 0 85223 139 3

Consultant editor: John Wright
House editor: Isabel Sutherland
Designer: Derek Morrison
Cover photograph: Kenneth Scowen

Filmset and printed in Great Britain by
BAS Printers Limited, Over Wallop, Hampshire
and bound by
Cambridge University Press, Cambridge

Contents

Acknowledgments

I should like to give my grateful thanks to my Consultant Editor, John Wright, for his unstinting help and advice, and for contributing the chapter on *Routine Care in the Greenhouse*.

Also to Donald Johnson, who wrote the final section on *Choosing, Installing and Equipping Your Greenhouse*, and who has a masterful approach to such matters which eludes me!

Sheila Howarth

Introduction

The idea of devoting your greenhouse primarily to producing things you can eat is in a way a complete reversal of its old fashioned use for growing pot plants, bedding plants, tender shrubs, chrysanthemums, cacti and so on. But it is a trend that is very much in the spirit of today. Anyone who has in recent years discovered the joys and rewards of growing food crops rather than – or alongside – flowers will need no convincing of the enormously increased range of possibilities that are available to the greenhouse owner.

When you buy a greenhouse with the intention of growing your own food you are investing in something intangible and at the same time far too elusive to be bought . . . flavour and freedom to choose. The other benefits are convenience, and above all, economy. Each household will have its own priority . . . early crops; rare crops; and everyday 'tender' crops such as annual herbs and salads. Obviously you cannot, in a modest-sized greenhouse, hope to grow all or even the majority of the crops that are included in this book – both for reasons of space and because the very wide range of fruit and vegetables covered need widely varying conditions. To help you choose among the combinations of crops that have similar needs, an indication is given under individual crops of other crops that can be grown with them.

The special appeal of crops grown in a greenhouse is that everything you eat is truly fresh. You pick the crops at their ultimate moment of flavour, some young, such as cucumbers, others bursting with ripeness, like figs. Whatever the crop, it will not have endured a long journey, or been tiered-up in a sunny display till it is bought by the undiscerning. Its life should be straight from the plant to the pot or the deep freeze.

Freedom to choose just what varieties you want is yet another bonus. You can raise and sustain your own plants grown from seed with just sun heat if you like. Instead of buying young plants raised by a commercial nurseryman, when you are limited to *his* choice, which will, from necessity be produced for reliability, appearance, travel endurance . . . rather than flavour. How often can you buy the fruit of, or even the plants of yellow tomatoes? Only if you grow them for yourself from seed.

A greenhouse is not a luxury. It is basically a shelter, giving maximum light and sun and protection from winds and downpours, so that the tender-hearted plants can remain there permanently, and seedlings can be raised and protected until they are sufficiently weather-proof to be put into the open ground. Greenhouses are usually classified into three categories according to the span of temperatures of the artificial climate created within them.

Introduction

An unheated, or cold, greenhouse is what it says – and though capable of keeping out slight frost of short duration is unreliable early in the spring. The use of a heated propagator increases its usefulness but it is not sensible to plant crops with a relatively high temperature requirement – such as cucumbers – until perhaps early May.

A cool greenhouse is one where perhaps a night minimum temperature of 4°C (40°F) is maintained. This is more expensive to run than the unheated house. It brings forward the date when tender plants can be put out in it but they will not thrive in a cold spring.

The fully heated greenhouse is expensive to run but enables you to grow the full range of crops described here without any difficulties.

Most vegetable and fruit crops grow happily in the open throughout the year and produce their crops at their natural season. However, to steal a march on fellow growers you need controllable warmth early in the season; then you can produce food throughout the year. After putting out the indoor raised seedlings when the air and soil are warm, keep inside during summer only tender plants which will sulk if left out on a cold night. These include half-hardy herbs, and exotic fruit and vegetables requiring tropical conditions.

You can start the eating year by forcing the crops of the previous season which have been grown in open ground – rhubarb and chicory – and for the gourmet who can take a little extra trouble, seakale. Follow with extra early potatoes, then choose between early sowings of celery, peas, French beans, early cauliflowers, vegetable marrows, to be put into the open ground later. This leaves the summer greenhouse for tomatoes, cucumbers, melons, sweet peppers (capsicums), aubergines (eggplant), and golden berry (edible Chinese lanterns).

Other fruit can be grown permanently under glass if you have a particular passion. A lean-to against a good length of wall is best for fig, nectarine, peach, passion fruit and grape, in a part of the country where they will not fruit in the open. You may prefer to give major space to these luxury crops at the expense of everyday, easily bought ones, but do remember that the space required by a grapevine, for instance, is considerable. And even if you decide that you cannot spare room for these traditional luxuries of the Victorian conservatory, you may be tempted to find a corner for one of the more unusual 'fun' crops included here, such as passion fruit.

It's as well to recognize from the start that a greenhouse *is* a commitment, though a very rewarding and worthwhile one. It will make demands on your time and patience and it is essential to have a clear idea of what you're letting yourself in for before you decide on one. The model that attracts you in advertisements, or a special offer, may need the enthusiasm and single-mindedness of a far more devoted grower than yourself. Remember that holidays can be a problem, unless you have installed various automatic devices, or have an understanding neighbour or living-in friends. Detailed advice on choosing, erecting and equipping a greenhouse is given in the final section. Here are a few points to consider. Does it have glass to the ground? Is it adequately ventilated? easy to erect? And if you're intending to have a heated house, it is a sensible precaution to check that big panes of glass are adequately sealed.

The aim of this book is to provide anyone new to greenhouse gardening with all the basic information needed to grow fruit and vegetables in a small space, at a small cost, and with the least effort.

The first part is about fruit and vegetables growing permanently (some in succession) in the greenhouse. Next come the forced crops – rhubarb, chicory, seakale – which are brought inside from the cold for a brief coddling. Then we show you how to raise seed in the greenhouse for crops which will be grown on outdoors, using it as a nursery. Thus the inter-dependence of greenhouse and garden makes a perfect working combination, particularly with the addition of such aids as those resting and readjusting homes, frames and cloches. Part 2 also includes the regular care and general running of your greenhouse.

The facts you need to know when making the initial investment are put before you in the final part, which includes detailed advice on the choice of specialized equipment from staging to watering systems, *ie*, the furnishings of your greenhouse.

Basic Equipment

All that is absolutely necessary to start off with, is staging, pots, pans, compost, an old kitchen knife, fork and spoon, your chosen seeds and a watering can. The niceties you add to these basics will depend on what you choose to grow, with or without heat; what you consider worth spending money on, and what you can do without. We all have our individual priorities.

Many of the things you need can be found idling around the house, unused, and purloined. Others can be made very easily from odds and ends, like the presser; or knocked together from scrap pieces of wood, such as the handy little portable potting tray shown in the drawing below, along with some other items described in this chapter.

Bucket The general dogsbody in and out of the greenhouse. Two at least, one small, one large, for mixing composts, washing vegetables, and equipment. Have them with marked measures and a lip for mixing liquid and dry feeds to be poured into smaller containers.

Compost It is not an economy to use garden soil for propagation but rather buy compost which should have been sterilized. This gives freedom from weed seeds, pests and diseases and will have balanced nutrients added to make it suitable for either seed sowing or growing on (usually sold as a potting mixture). John Innes compost, based on clay loam, is quite satisfactory and usually cheaper than one of the proprietary peat-based mixtures, which can be more difficult to water. The appearance of this compost does not vary much whether it is wet or dry, whereas a soil-based compost changes colour and indicates the need for watering. Old compost stores well in unopened or re-sealed bags if kept dry.

1

Basic Equipment

Dibber This is a pointed, short wooden tool used for making holes both deep and shallow for seeds and planting out seedlings. To make a wider hole for such customers as leeks and parsnips, the dibber when plunged in at the required depth can be gently moved from side to side. It can be made from any broken broom or tool handle, or cut from a pruned tree or hedgerow, trimmed to a length which suits your back – usually about one foot. Round off the point so that it is blunt. A pencil-sharp tip can leave an airspace below the seed or seedling destined for their man-made pits, which kills them if they cannot make contact with surrounding soil moisture. Cut ridges in the dibber from the point upwards, marking the depths like a ruler (*see drawing 1*).

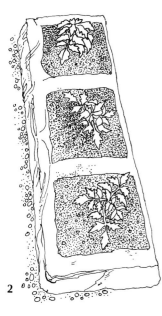

Growing bags These contain specially formulated compost. They are easy, clean, and can be arranged on greenhouse bench, staging, or on balconies or patios. They are particularly useful for bringing up tomatoes, sweet peppers, aubergines, cucumbers, strawberries, herbs, salads and melons. No seed must be sown directly into the compost. Always follow the instructions on the bags as to watering, planting and general maintenance. Be particularly careful when staking plants, or giving them support which might pierce the bottom of the bags. If the floor of the house is, for instance 'tomato sick' then to pierce the bag will let the roots grow out into infected soil. If not, piercing the bag will improve drainage and let roots grow into the border, reducing the need for very frequent watering in hot weather.

Never try to re-use the compost in the greenhouse at the end of the growing season. Tip it onto the compost heap or dig it into the garden. Growing bags are rather costly, but save time, space and are efficient. They also avoid the need to replace soil in the floor of the greenhouse if this has been used for cropping for several seasons (*see drawing 2*).

Labels A matter of personal taste and convenience. There are all sizes and shapes in metal, plastic and wood, or if you want to be extravagant, there are hand machines for making your own – a great advantage if you are unable to read your own handwriting. For temporary use, stiff scrap paper such as the backs of greeting cards can be tucked under boxes or in a cleft twig or thin cane. Woody shrub prunings and the stiff dead stems of perennial flowers can be used for this purpose. Aluminium labels are probably the most long-lasting and useful of all. Alternatively, wooden labels can be cut to size with a penknife from any thin scrap of wood, like fruit or lettuce containers, whitewashed and repainted whenever they are re-used.

Maximum and minimum thermometer An essential item of equipment so you can see at a glance, instead of relying on your personal feeling of hot and cold, what the temperature is currently and has been. From the many types, choose the one you can read most easily.

Measure This again can be a kitchen cast-off. A measure is essential for correct doses of feeds, insecticides and assorted killers. Most of the liquid

13

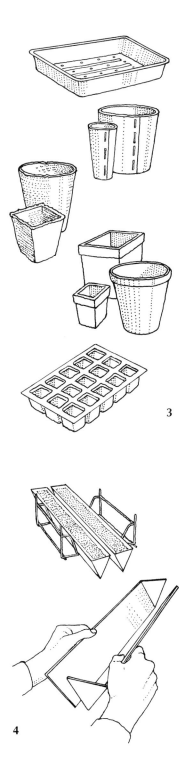

products have a screw cap designed to double as a measure, but you will still need a larger jug or bucket for adding the appropriate amount of water. Make sure the measure marks are clearly visible on both inside and out. If you have to lift it up to the light with a shaky hand you can well administer an overdose. Two measures, a small and a large measure are more convenient and if you can't trust yourself to be careful about cleaning and drying, have one exclusively for measuring dry powders or grains.

Pots and containers Plastic pots and trays have the advantage of being lighter and easier to clean and store and are cheaper than clay, but on the debit side you have to be much more wary when watering. The plants in them can easily become waterlogged and their roots drowned, whereas clay pots would absorb the extra, unwanted moisture, and gradually release it. Peat, paper and whalehide pots can be used as lodgings before plants are put out (*see drawing 3*).

Presser A piece of wood used for firming and levelling compost before and after sowing the seeds. It needs a short handle or knob on top and should fit just inside the rim of the container. It can be round or rectangular to fit any of your pots and pans. What household cannot disgorge an old cupboard knob or handle, put in the tool drawer because it might come in useful?

3

Seed boxes Plastic has largely taken over here, as plastic boxes are lighter and easier to clean, but the advantages are minimized by their tendency to crack at the lips; also, they are not rigid when they have to be transferred from one place to another while weighted down with damp compost. The main advantage is that they retain moisture longer because they are not porous. An ingenious new 'take apart' triangular seed trough (*see drawing 4*) solves the problem of transplanting seedlings, such as those of root crops, which don't take kindly to root disturbance. It enables seeds to be grown in compost on the greenhouse staging and when ready for transplanting, the trough is lifted bodily and placed in a V-shaped furrow in the garden soil and the sections slid clear.

Sieves For most purposes of potting and seed sowing use a 1-cm (3/8-in) mesh, with a finer one for lightly covering the seeds. Whoever's in charge of the kitchen in your household is usually only too willing to part with an old one as an excuse to buy a new and better version.

4

Sprayers A great variety to choose from and you will need at least two (*see drawing 5*). They are essential for the control of pests and disease, and for spraying plants in hot weather. A small hand spray is invaluable, with a larger one for general purposes, which can be pumped or pressurized. There is a wide price range so choose the best you can afford for the job you want it to do. Nothing is worse value and does more damage to the temper than a blocked or reluctant sprayer, or an exuberant one which sprays you from its joints. Unless you are a

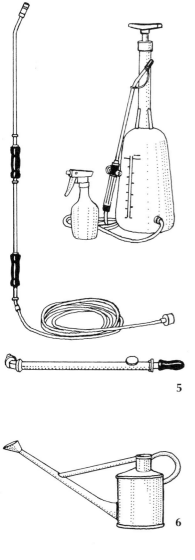

permanently reliable washer-out of garden containers, keep separately labelled ones for pests, disease and clear water. Never attempt to keep left over chemicals after mixing them up and never, ever leave chemicals, labelled or unlabelled, where a child, or a confused elderly person has access to them.

Ties Fillis, a type of brown string, is a great standby, obtainable in different thicknesses for different purposes, or there are plastic covered wire twisters, flat paperbound ones such as deep-freeze ties, and raffia, twine, and split rings. Some can be bought in a reel so they can be cut to your own lengths. Raffia is the cheapest and gentlest on the plants (soak for a few hours before using), but is expendable. The others can be reused many times.

Watering-can Plastic ones are lighter, usually last longer and are cheaper than metal ones. The choice is personal. They are in many shapes and sizes, with the spouts long and short, at differing angles, with many shapes and sizes of hole, rose-nozzle and of top opening. Never buy one on appearance. It must be well balanced. A good garden shop should allow you to try the one you choose, preferably filled, before you decide on it. Points to remember are: your own height and carrying strength; the length of spout needed to reach the back plants on a bed or bench; how far you have to carry the water and the weight you can lift; and whether the handle and the bar joining the spout to the top of the can are comfortable for your height and arm length (*see drawing 6*). This is all part of getting the balance right for your size, the height the can has to be lifted, and the distance the spray has to reach. It is an advantage to have fine, coarse and medium rose attachments, but these may not be easily available if you opt for a plastic rather than a metal can.

Note Staging and other 'furnishings', together with equipment for heating, ventilating and watering, are dealt with in the final section.

5

6

Part 1

How to Grow
All Kinds of Fruit
and Vegetables

Like other types of gardening, return from the greenhouse depends on the effort put into it. A carefully worked out schedule of cropping will give greater variety of produce over a longer period, but at greater effort and attention to detail than if the house is used for a simple rotation. This will, almost certainly, produce more than the average household can use at times of maximum production.

Since all crops have slightly different requirements for temperature and humidity, most mixed cropping, with the house used to grow two crops at the same time, is often not ideal for either and unless greenhouse dividers are used the beginner risks disappointment if each crop is not given the conditions it needs. It may be easier until experience has been gained to start with a simple rotation, adding as experience grows.

Commonly grown crops with contrasting needs are the tomato (lower temperatures, dryer atmosphere) and cucumber (higher temperature and humidity). Each can, however, be grown with crops with similar requirements; sweet peppers or capsicums like the conditions suited to tomatoes and melons prefer a cucumber atmosphere at least until fruit ripening. Under the following section dealing with the cultivation of individual crops are tables giving the conditions which suit them and also other crops which can share with them.

'Soil Sickness', Crop Rotations
One of the inevitable consequences of growing crops in the soil in the floor of the house is that of 'soil sickness' usually resulting from a build-up of pests, diseases and possibly fertilizer residues as well as waste products from plant roots. While the precise causes are often obscure the reduction in cropping after several years of tomatoes, for instance, is all too obvious. Many of the ways of avoiding this problem are not attractive; chemicals for partial soil sterilization are not very effective. Re-soiling the house is impossible for many people. Ring culture, that is, covering affected soil with weathered ash and growing crops in rings of compost, developing two root systems, one absorbing water from the ash, the other nutrients from the compost in the ring, limits the use of the house to crops which can be grown by this method. Growing bags are the big breakthrough, which enable crops to be grown out of contact with the soil of the house, but they

do have certain disadvantages, apart from cost and are not entirely plain sailing particularly as to watering.

These comments are not intended to emphasize the difficulties of greenhouse cropping, but so that the new greenhouse owner can plan to meet them. What can you do to reduce the risk of soil sickness? Rotate crops round the house where possible. Grow in soil in the floor for as long as crops are satisfactory. Grow carefully, avoiding excesses of fertilizer and be particularly watchful over plants which die. These should be carefully removed, with some soil from the border if in doubt as to whether the disease is likely to spread. When plant growth becomes less vigorous and before cropping has declined too badly, then grow in containers.

Cultivating instructions for individual crops are given in the following pages. But before you embark on your first heady venture into greenhouse gardening, do please read the chapter on *Routine Care in the Greenhouse*; this goes into greater detail about the points which have been touched on briefly above.

Two Popular Crops

Tomatoes

Sow	Plant	Position	Harvest from	Propa-gation	Temperatures Night min.	Day max.	Notes
mid-Jan.	mid-April	floor of greenhouse or 17 cm (7 in) pots	early–mid June	16–18°C (60–65°F)	16°C (60°F)	23°C (74°F)	Can be grown alongside any other plant which requires fairly dry growing conditions. This includes pepper and aubergine.
late Feb.	late April	floor of greenhouse or 17 cm (7 in) pots	July–August	as above	can be grown without heat	23°C (74°F)	Cropping then delayed into August.
mid-March	Indoors early May outdoors mid–late May	as above	Aug.–Sept. Sept.	as above	as above	23°C (74°F)	Should not be planted out until all risk of frost is over.

Any greenhouse whether heated or not will grow tomatoes. Many people buy their first one primarily to supply the family with this most popular crop. Bought ones, however fresh, can never compete with the smell and taste of those picked and eaten straight from the plant. In growing habit there is a choice of types, the fruit ranging in size from that of a cherry to giants weighing as much as half a kilo (around a pound); and in colour from bright red to yellow, golden, striped red and yellow and striped green and red. Tomatoes need only reasonable warmth.

By raising your own seed you can entirely please yourself about varieties, and avoid any aimed at the commercial market, which implies they are good travellers rather than eaters. Even a small packet of seeds will produce more plants than you will have space for in the greenhouse. If you want to grow several varieties, arrange a swap with other greenhouse friends, and each grow a different kind. Or you could sell the surplus plants, hardened off, to neighbours without one, to grow in frames, under cloches or in the open. Even if the unwanted seedlings end on the compost heap overall the ones used will have cost considerably less than bought, hardened-off plants from a nursery. Or the surplus plants can take their chance out of doors if you have the space. Even varieties specially recommended for indoor growing can do surprisingly well outdoors in our unpredictable summers.

Growing methods
The normal habit of the tomato is to sprawl on the ground, producing a bush. It is usually trained up canes or strings and the side shoots removed.

The plants can be grown, according to choice, in the border soil of the greenhouse; in large pots or boxes; in plastic bags filled with compost (growing bags); or by ring culture. Each has good points as well as slight drawbacks which can make you favour one rather than another.

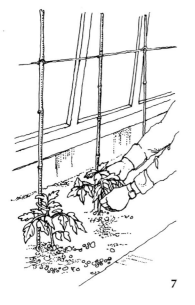

7

Borders This is the traditional method of growing by setting the plants directly into the soil, which cuts down the amount of watering and feeding to be done. The drawback is that you risk more diseases and pests through soil deterioration, if the tomato is grown in border soil year after year, and the soil is rather slow to warm up in spring even in a gently heated house. Dig in plenty of well-rotted manure or peat before planting. Top with a sprinkle of sulphate of potash mixed with an organic fertilizer, at 100 g (4 oz) to the square yard, or to the instructions of the manufacturer. Space the plants about 50 cm (18 in) apart unless the seed packet directions say differently. Some of the dwarf bush varieties can be much closer. (See *drawing 7.*)

Pots and boxes Growing the plants in sterilized potting compost gives them a good start in life, free from the diseases which can occur in border soil which has carried several crops of tomatoes. The pots should be 22 cm (9 in) in size and the boxes any convenient size to hold one or more plants at the appropriate spacing. The containers can stand on the border soil 30–35 cm (12–14 in) apart, or directly onto solid flooring. In very hot weather, moist peat packed around or under them, will help to maintain moisture around the plants. The only drawback is that they need very careful watering during their early growing life to get the proper balance between top and root growth. You must be sparing rather than generous. Plants in full growth where rooting is not permitted into the border need more frequent watering in hot weather.

Growing bags An expensive method but labour-saving as they avoid having to replace the soil in the floor of the house because it will no longer grow satisfactory crops. They look like plastic pillows and are ready-filled with peat-based compost. The only effort required is to lay them flat on soil or solid floor, slit them in marked places (usually three), put in the plants, follow the watering and growing instructions provided, and give them some support, unless they are a bush type. The drawback is that their usefulness ends with the life of the plants. You can tip the used-up compost on to the garden to improve soil structure or use it for propagating plants other than tomato in following seasons. You have to buy new bags for the next season. There is no sense in mixing your own compost and refilling the bags. It is a complicated and far from labour-saving task for an amateur. If you had the resolve you could have done it in the first place and used the compost in pots, saving the expense of bags. (See *drawing on page 13.*)

Ring culture One of the alternative ways of growing tomatoes, in bottomless pots or rings where border soil has been growing tomato crops for several years and soil problems have built up, resulting in

20

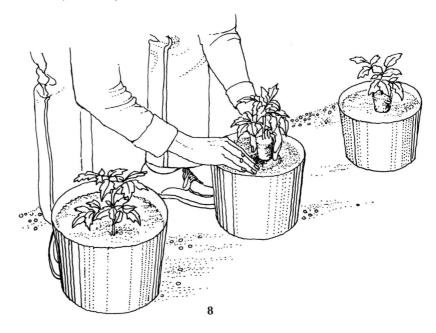

8

poor growth and yield. These rings are usually made of plastic or bituminized paper, with a minimum depth and diameter of 22 cm (9 in), and stand on top of a 10–15 cm (4–6 in) layer of inert material such as weathered ashes or gravel. The object of this method is to contain the fine feeding roots of the plant to the pot where they are fed regularly, and a second, coarser system of roots works its way down into the aggregate and takes up water. (*See drawings 8 and 9.*)

The advantage of ring culture is that very little fresh compost is needed each year; plant growth is easy to control, and the small amount of growing medium is fully exposed to the warmth. They will though, need large quantities of water, particularly in mid-summer. But this is not necessarily a disadvantage, unless you have to carry water from a distance, as it is given only to the aggregate. However thirsty the compost in the rings seems to be, don't be tempted to give them a drip of water. The idea is to keep the food concentrated in the ring rather than wash it away. There are entire books devoted to this technique with all its niceties (and nasties) for those who become hooked on it. Briefly, to

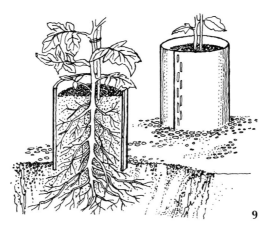

9

shortcut these: stand the rings 50 cm (18 in) apart on whatever aggregate you choose, partly fill them with potting compost (John Innes No 3), and transfer the seedlings before they have completely filled their 9 cm (3 ½ in) pots with roots. Top up with compost to within 2–3 cm (1 in) of the rim of the ring, then water only once to settle the feeding roots and encourage them quickly to send down coarser water-seeking roots into the aggregate which should be watered regularly with plain water right from the start. Begin feeding the roots in the ring when the first fruits have set on the bottom truss of flowers.

Sowing

Tomato seeds will not thank you for hurrying them from a cosy packet to a cold seed tray, for them like leaving a feather bed for a park bench. Once they are in the mood and the right conditions to get going, they resent any discomfort which can interrupt their performance; such as a cold spring.

It is a waste of time to sow too early. They take 6–8 weeks from sowing to their final planting. To germinate well they need a temperature of 16–18°C (60–65°F) and it is economical to raise them in a propagator. Mid-March is quite early enough to sow for the plants to go into their selected greenhouse positions at the beginning of May, if your greenhouse is unheated and you are prepared to forgo early crops. Tomatoes grow much better when the days are longer. Beginner gardeners usually sow their seed in February and early March, hoping to steal a march over expensive imported ones. For the cost of maintaining the high temperature at that time of year to get germination, they would do better to buy the fruit, or plants raised in a good local nursery.

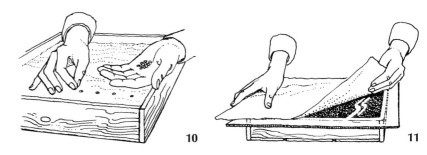

10   11

Sow seeds thinly into seed trays or 13 cm (5 in) pots of seed compost. Space the seeds about 1 cm (½ in) apart (see *drawing 10*); overcrowded seedlings become spindly. Sprinkle a covering of compost and water lightly. If you have an unheated greenhouse and no propagator, you can start off the seeds in an airing cupboard, or anywhere in the house which will provide a steady temperature as given above. The containers should be sealed in polythene bags, or covered with dark paper and a sheet of glass to keep in the moisture. Take a peep at them twice a day, for as soon as they nose through they must be put into full light so they do not become drawn and leggy. (See *drawing 11*.)

A germination temperature over 18°C (65°F) may produce quicker growth, but also some seedlings which bear no fruit when the plants

12

grow up. Germination takes place about a week after sowing, and a few days later seedlings are big enough to be transferred singly into pots containing potting compost . . . 7–11 cm (3–4½ in) are the usual size. Be tender when handling these tiny seedlings; never touch the stem, only hold by a leaf (*see drawing 12*). They now need a temperature of 16°C (60°F), and must be well watered.

When at least one flower opens on the first truss of buds, they are ready for planting out by whichever method you have chosen.

The sowing method is the same if the plants are to be grown outdoors in warm and sheltered areas, but the timing is different. Seed sown in mid-March produces plants ready for planting outside by the middle or later part of May, when they have been hardened off by gradually getting them used to outdoor temperatures by standing them in a cold frame.

Feeding

This needs the commonsense of a mother and the knowledge of a doctor. Throw away all the books on baby care . . . diagnose the symptoms, then apply the correct prescription whenever the plants do not look 'themselves'. In general, lush and leggy ones, making too much growth, need potash; stunted ones are crying out for more nitrogen.

There are many ways of regular feeding. Do what is most convenient for you and the growing method you are using. Buy one of the excellent proprietary foods (fertilizers) and use *exactly* as the directions say. Manufacturers spend many years and fortunes experimenting, to get the balance just right, so that you don't have to guess. If you are going to be mingy or over generous, you will do more harm than good to the plants.

Unless the young plants are obviously pining for nourishment, do not give any feed until the first truss of fruit is set and the young tomatoes are about the size of a pea.

Air and heat

Temperatures obviously vary with the weather and amount of ventilation you allow. To produce the best fruit, they need about 18°C (65°F) by day and 16°C (60°F) at night. Open the ventilators when the temperature reaches 21°C–23°C (70°F–74°F) but beware of draughts.

Supports

Provide these as soon as possible after the plants are in their permanent homes. You can use stakes or canes tall enough to reach the roof if you prefer, but the most effective way is up a string. This is anchored to a stake or hooked galvanized wire pushed into the soil close to each plant. Leaving some slack, which can be tightened later if the plants sag, tie the string to tight horizontal wires, or a hook in the roofing bar, but make sure first that the roof can bear the weight of the crop. As the plants develop, wind the main stem clockwise around the string, about twice a week, with careful fingers – the stem snaps easily. Make sure the leaves are not trapped and that the string does not throttle any newly forming flower truss. (*See drawings 13 and 14.*)

13

Growing bags should be staked with caution, or you may penetrate the plastic pillow at ground level. This will allow roots to grow through into border soil which may be harmful to plant growth if that soil is already 'tomato sick'. This extra root will ease watering in high summer, however. They can be put against a trellis of wire or wood, or you can buy special metal frames to go with them.

Layering A problem with many houses is the limited height in which crops can grow. Placing plants on the border gives even more restricted headroom. To give more growing space, the plants can be 'layered'. This means that when they are almost touching the roof the strings to which plants are attached are untied at the roof end and the stem laid along the ground and re-attached further along the house so the growing point is 30–60 cm (1–2 ft) above soil level. Then more growth can be made without the top of the house becoming overcrowded with shoots. This operation can result in fruit being laid on the soil where it will be splashed during watering. Cover the soil with straw to keep the fruit clean. In anticipation of this method of training, the length of the string used to support each plant should be longer than usual. (*See drawing 15*).

14

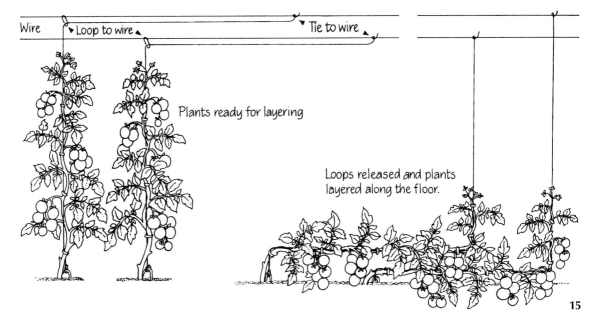

Wire   Loop to wire   Tie to wire

Plants ready for layering

Loops released and plants layered along the floor.

15

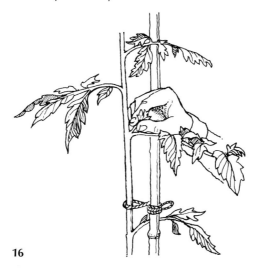

16

Maintenance

Tomatoes grown on a single stem produce side shoots where the leaf stalk joins the stem. These must be pinched out by hand (*see drawing 16*) as soon as they appear; if allowed to escape, and grow, they will sap strength from the plant and reduce cropping. Unless layering is planned, the plants are 'stopped' by nipping out the tips of the main stems when they are reaching the roof. By then they should have formed eight or more trusses of fruit if grown in the border soil. Those grown in pots or boxes should be stopped at six trusses. (*See drawing 16.*)

There is no truth in the popular belief that removing the lower leaves of tomatoes helps to ripen the fruit, in the sun. They will willingly ripen under the shade of leaves (or even picked green in autumn and kept in frost-free places, till Christmas). Plant nutrition depends on the leaves, and it is they who need the sun. So be cautious about removing any healthy leaves, particularly those above a fruit truss. If leaves do yellow, cut them off cleanly close to the main stem. Exposed directly to the sunlight, the flesh of the fruit can become hardened, an unpleasant complaint known as 'greenback'. We must all have been sold such duds at times. They feel firm, and when cut in half look like a fossil. The reason to remove leaves is that mature plants become overcrowded with them, and they block the flow of air. Otherwise take off only leaves which are yellow or diseased. Bush types can be left to themselves, though you may wish to keep low trusses clean with some straw under them.

Pollination

This should happen in the normal events of plant life in a temperature of around 21°C (70°F). But in the early part of the growing season, March to May, greenhouse temperatures do not encourage flower pollination. The simple remedy is to hand-pollinate by tapping the flower trusses lightly, to stir the pollen around. This should be done daily. On sunny days a jet of water directly aimed at the flowers will both shake them and go on to produce the humid conditions which are near ideal for fertilization.

Harvesting

Pick the fruit just when you want to eat it. This is a judgement of personal taste. A fully ripe fruit will snap cleanly from the truss, complete with the green calyx. These will keep well if they must. Windowsill ripening is no quicker than leaving the fruit on the plant, and the flavour vanishes. Some of the new varieties, particularly for salads, are at their best when green, with a slight blush, and their insides a mint and pink colour.

Hazards

Irregular watering (letting the plants dry out at some stage) causes 'blossom end rot' which creates a sunken black area at the base of the fruit. Make watering more regular. Too much direct sunlight hardens the flesh causing 'greenback'.

Leafmould is caused by poor ventilation although many modern varieties are resistant. Spray at once with a copper fungicide and adjust the ventilation.

White fly can appear in spite of your sticking to all the rules. They are easily destroyed with smoke pellets or by spraying the underside of the leaves with liquid malathion.

Potato blight will turn the leaves and fruit brown. At the first sign, or as a preventative, spray with Bordeaux mixture from early July.

Aphids are occasionally a problem and can be cured with smokes containing HCH.

Recommended varieties

Don't squander your greenhouse by filling it with everyday commercial varieties you can buy in any shop. You gain little but saving a few pence. It is a misuse of the greenhouse unless it can be the protector and provider of something special. Some of those recommended can be grown equally well indoors and out once hardened off, which will be determined by the space you have, and the quantity you want to grow. Any surplus freeze extremely well raw and whole, or made into purée, which can keep you going a whole year.

Big Boy (greenhouse only.) An almost vulgar (overwhelming) crop of fruit weighing from 0·5 kg (1 lb) to 0·9 kg (2 lb) each. They have a thick meaty flesh with a fine flavour. Ideal for sandwiches, or sliced as a salad with a French dressing.

Gardener's Delight Praised by many gourmets as being top of the tomato tree for flavour. The fruit is not large but exceptionally sweet and excellent in sandwiches and salads. Suitable for outdoors.

Golden Sunrise Butter yellow, they have a rare, exquisite flavour, which is particularly enjoyed by children, who often seem to prefer them to stone fruit such as cherries and plums. Suitable for outdoors.

Pixie A 60 cm (2 ft) bush which will carry up to 30 fast-ripening trusses. Excellent flavour. Can be grown in pots, but may need some cane support because of its very heavy crop. Suitable for outdoors, under cloches.

Super Roma The Italian plum tomato grown entirely for cooking. It is deep red, thick, juicy, almost seedless and shaped like a long plum. Disease resistant with a full, tangy flavour, it is used for sauces, soups, purées and ketchup.

Sweet 100 Produces a colossal number of 2·5 cm (1 in) diameter fruit of bite-size, with such a sweet flavour you can eat them as you would strawberries. Bearing such a heavy crop it must be well staked, and the side shoots removed. The plants continue cropping heavily until frost. Their size makes them perfect for using whole and unpeeled, tossed with lettuce or a mixed dressed salad, or cooked on top of savoury tarts, such as egg, cheese and bacon, or fish pies.

Tigerella (Mr Stripey). A very early variety, both in and out of the greenhouse, and completely free of 'greenback' trouble. It has a unique rich tangy flavour, and clearly marked yellow and red stripes. Some people prefer to eat it under-ripe. Suitable for outdoors.

Cucumbers

Sow	Plant	Position	Harvest from	Temperatures			Notes
				Propagation	Night min.	Day max.	
early Feb. onwards	early Mar.	beds on house floor; also pots, boxes or growing bags	early May	24°C (75°F)	18°C (65°F)	24°C (75°F)	Ideal conditions for cucumber are too humid and warm for many other crops.
early March	early April	beds on house floor	mid June		as above		

Cucumbers are remarkably easy to grow, and will overwhelm a small greenhouse, as well as your capacity to eat them, if you put in too many plants. There are two main types, the greenhouse or frame, which grow under glass; and ridge, which can be germinated indoors and put in the open when frosts are over, or the seed put in where they are to grow outside when the ground has warmed up. They will need no transplanting.

The biggest and best crops for flavour and tenderness are produced in the greenhouse, where there is also less risk of cross-pollination. This happens when the male flowers are not removed at an early stage, and the resulting fruit from the female flowers are bitter and useless.

Methods of growing
They need to be grown under hotter, more humid conditions than tomatoes and must not be grown among plants needing airy, dryer and cooler conditions. The growing positions are the same as for tomatoes: in

17   18

beds on the border soil, in pots (*see drawings 17 and 18*), boxes or growing bags. Or the seedlings, after being hardened off, can be planted outside under cloches, or with no protection at all, depending on the particular variety you choose. All a matter of convenience.

Sowing
From February onwards sow the seeds edgeways, just below the surface, singly into 7.5 cm (3 in) pots of seed compost kept at 24°C (75°F); after germination they must have a humid temperature which is never less than 18–21°C (65–70°F). Germination takes only a few days and the seedlings must be watered freely. It takes 5–6 weeks from sowing to the final planting, which, with ordinary varieties is at the four leaf stage. It is important not to have any check to growth at any stage.

Planting
Large pots or boxes are filled with a good potting compost such as John Innes No 3 and put on the staging or floor. These will need more care in watering and general supervision than those in borders. The beds must be prepared in advance, giving good drainage by forking in strawy manure, or a rich potting compost. Make a low, broad ridge, about 40 cm (15 in) wide and 17 cm (7 in) deep and set the plants at least 60 cm (2 ft) apart, with the soil ball just slightly above the surface.

Supports
These are needed at once as the growth needs constant tying in. Simply train the main stem as you would tomatoes, up bamboo canes, wire or string.

Training and maintenance
As the laterals (side shoots) form, pinch out the tip at one leaf beyond the

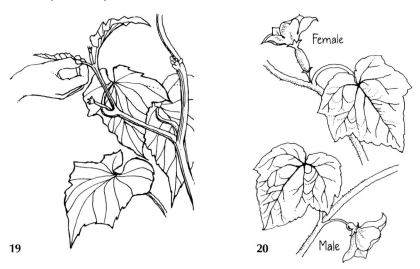

19   **20**

first fruit (*see drawing 19*). When the plant reaches the roof, or as far as you intend, snip off the growing point of the main stem.

On many varieties, both male and female flowers will form. All male blooms must be nipped in the bud, as it were, to prevent fertilization of the females, as this would cause the fruit to be misshapen, due to the presence of seeds, and bitter. The female flowers are easy to tell; they have an embryo fruit just behind the petals (*see drawing 20*). Some newer varieties only produce female flowers. It is generally thought best not to allow any fruit to form on the main stem but only on the laterals. Throughout their growing life cucumbers need moist, muggy conditions resembling those of a Turkish bath. This can be created with plenty of spraying, but is not necessarily to the comfort of other plants. A compromise can be reached by growing the cucumbers at the end of the greenhouse opposite the door, leaving the more airy and cooler space for those which take deeper breaths.

Feeding
When the white roots of the plants break through the surface of the ridge, topdress with a thin layer of the same compost in which they are growing.

Harvesting
Cucumbers grown in conditions just to their liking should be ready to eat within 12–14 weeks after the seed is sown. Cut them as soon as they are parallel-sided over their whole length. The flavour and texture are finer, and the plant will be encouraged to produce in greater abundance.

Hazards
Bitterness: the causes are uncertain but probably include checks in their growth usually due to low temperatures. A particular hazard is *gummosis*, a fungus which causes a gummy liquid to ooze from sunken spots on the fruits which can happen in dull, wet seasons (*see drawing 21*). Raise the temperature, give more ventilation, remove all the

21

29

affected fruit and dust the diseased plants regularly with zineb.
Powdery mildew caused usually by lack of ventilation. White powder
appears on leaves and shoot tips. There are now resistant varieties. Use a
systemic fungicide, such as thiophanate-methyl or dinocap spray or
dust.
Red spider causing white spotting on upper leaf surfaces. The minute
mites can also be seen on the under surfaces. Although chemical
spraying is possible the mites are encouraged by hot dry conditions and
the best control is by spraying plants more liberally with water.

Recommended varieties

Choice is wide and varied in shape, colour and behaviour, from the
'burpless' which are ridge types and which wander around outside
unaided, until crippled by frost, to the all-female, labour-saving
greenhouse varieties newly introduced.

Fertila (greenhouse or frame.) Has no male flowers so is free from risk of
pollination and as a bonus is resistant to gummosis. Heavy cropper of
ideal length and colour.

Topsy (greenhouse.) Produces all-female flowers, which results in a huge
crop, but is remarkably sweet and juicy. Fruit is 20–40 cm (12–16 in) long
and slim.

Uniflora D (greenhouse.) A remarkable breakthrough in cucumber
breeding, which does its own training. All female plants have until now
needed much attention, tying up, pinching out and taking off leaves.
Uniflora D looks after itself, apart from needing some support. After
making its first side shoots, all other laterals stop short at about 15 cm
(6 in). This results in a crop over six months of up to 50 quality fruit.
Unlike other female types the foliage *must* be left on. You have little to do
but water, feed, and stand back.

Zeppelin (greenhouse or outdoors.) A giant fruit weighing 4·5–5·4 kg
(10–12 lb), which may sound too much of a good thing. But the
cucumbers stay ready for harvesting for a remarkably long period. When
picked green it is like normal varieties, but if left till a deep yellow it tastes
even better, and remains firm and juicy.

Some Delicious Fruit

Figs

Sow	Plant	Position	Harvest from	Propa-gation	Temperatures Night min.	Day max.	Notes
	start into growth Febr.	floor of house or large pot	August onwards		as for peach	as for peach	Almost as good results can be obtained by growing Fig against a wall in a favoured situation.

As can be plainly seen by anyone walking city pavements in England; fig trees abound . . . but their fruit does not. They are merely foliage plants. They love the warmth and restriction of their roots which paved streets and areas give them and the added warmth from the immense man-made activity going on below . . . underground trains, vast heating systems and hot and cold drainage from factories and hotels; and other unmentionable mysteries. Figs, then, are quite hardy in this country but the disadvantage is that the British fig tries here to do naturally what it does in its sub-tropical homes (the Middle East and Mediterranean countries) – ie, to produce two or three crops a year. Grown in the right position and given the correct root restriction, training and pruning, an outdoor fig will give a moderate crop of fruit in a good summer which starts early and ends late. These combinations being sadly rare, the greedy fig eater must hope to be satiated by greenhouse crops. With a little straight-jacket cruelty or in more pedestrian terms, root restriction, followed by understanding, figs need less attention than any other fruit, in or out of the greenhouse. With careful treatment you can bring two and even three crops to a mouth-watering ripeness each year.

Planting

The most vital lifeline to provide for a fig tree is good drainage and a permanent corset around the roots to prevent them from wandering off to make new leaf growths, instead of concentrating on providing for the fruit of the existing shoots. A sunny wall within the house is the perfect place. The border need be no more than 50 cm (1½ ft) wide from front to back. The cruelty referred to above consists of walling in the roots (see drawing 22 overleaf), to prevent them making more leaf than fruit.

Dig out the border, roughly 75 cm (2½ ft) square and deep . . . or wider if the wall area is large. Fill the bottom with 30 cm (12 in) of rubble . . . broken bricks, flint stones, mortar, and, in acid soils add some handfuls of chalk. Line the sides with bricks or concrete. Fill the rest of the space with

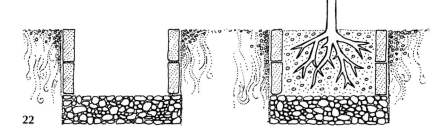

22

good loamy soil, and *no* manure. They must have a fertile, but never a rich soil. Corrugated iron, or an old water tank with the bottom pierced or removed, make easy substitutes. Good drainage is as important as enclosing the roots. Whatever restrictive practices you go in for, be careful not to create a bog, or the plant will drown. Young container-grown plants can be bought from specialist fruit nurseries and some garden centres. These can be planted at any time of year without disturbing the roots, though between November and February when they are dormant, they will need less attention.

Water and food

After correct planting, success with indoor figs depends very largely on watering . . . they need torrents at certain times, and never must those walled-in roots be allowed to dry out completely; though in winter they will not ask for much more than to be kept moist. In the spring when growth starts the borders should be watered every few days. When the days lengthen and are sunny the border may lap up a daily drench, and the foliage an early morning and evening showerbath. Stop the spraying when the first crop starts to ripen; give no food and water sparsely. Give an annual top-dressing of potash when the leaves and first-crop baby fruits start to show *after* removing the old dressing.

Pruning

This can be either very complicated or simple, according to your nature and purpose. You have figs forming at all stages; embryos and ripening fruit on the same branch, at the tips (*see drawing 23*); in the axils (where the base of a leaf shoots from the main stem) and along new shoots made the year before. Therefore the shorter the gap between each leaf, the more figs you will get. If the leaves grow up the stem more than 7·5 cm (3 in) apart the tree is growing too well, and you must be severe with rampant fruitless growth. The obvious course is to stop them from forming in the first place.

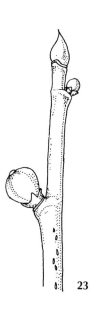

23

'Stopping' is done by rubbing off the tiny buds near the main stem of the tree, which are hoping to grow into branches. Do this throughout the growing season, by hand, as the mood takes you. There is no purpose in a violent, once-and-for-ever attack, as buds will keep forming. Leave enough to form where there are gaps, or to replace old ones, which must be cut out cleanly, preferably at leaf-fall when the sap will not bleed too seriously.

On no account leave a fig to its own devices. You are in charge and

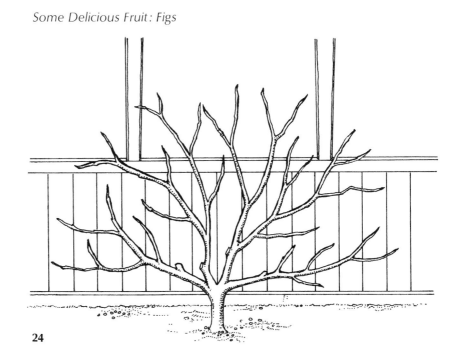

24

must limit it to the space available. A simple method of control is to nip out the growing tip of all mature shoots when they have produced five or six leaves. This will depend on the heat of the greenhouse and variety of fig grown. It could be as early as May. The most important point to understand is which figs are ever going to ripen, as the tree keeps producing embryos at all stages. Any sizable figs remaining on leafless branches in the autumn should be removed. At that time, the fruit which will ripen early for next year should be only the size of a small pea.

As the tree reaches the top of the greenhouse the fruit may become inconvenient to reach. To form fruiting branches lower down, from knee to eye level, annually shorten some of the older branches, or the convenient side shoots, to half their length and remove one or two branches completely, when the tree is leafless (*see drawing 24*).

Harvesting
Figs bend their necks, as though for the axe, when they are perfectly ripe, normally from August onwards and should stay on the tree until that ultimate moment and be eaten as soon as possible (*see drawing 25*). They should be bursting at the seams. Lift up the stems and break them off carefully.

Growing figs in pots
The yield will not be as large, or the tree as long-living, as those in open, though walled-in soil, but the great advantage is that the tree remains comparatively dwarf and can have a carefree outdoor summer, and then given greenhouse protection until the frosts are over. It also makes it easier to curb the exuberant root and leaf growth of those grown in soil.

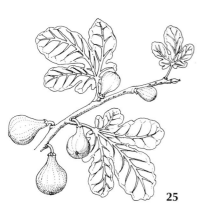

25

Plant the young fig tree in a 25–30 cm (10–12 in) pot in a fertile but not rich soil as you would for the border planted ones. Use John Innes potting compost No 1. Cover the drainage hole with a large piece of broken pot,

26

then a 3 cm (1 in) layer of smaller pieces or flints to make sure the roots are never in a bog. Ram the potting compost tightly around the roots as you pot it. Every year scrape away some of the soil from the top and replace with fresh compost (*see drawing 26*).

After three or four years knock the plant from its pot, gently shake off the old soil, trim the roots and put back into the same pot with fresh compost. Figs like a rest in the winter when the crop is finished and leaves begin to fall. Give no food, only enough water to keep them from drying out completely and keep them in an unheated greenhouse, or garage or shed. Too much warmth would have them struggling into leaf again, when they should be having a good nap. Prune in the same manner as border plants, though they will not want as much attention.

Recommended varieties

Bourjasotte Grise This is specially for the greenhouse, flat rather than round, with dark red flesh more syrupy and juicy than the others and very richly flavoured.

Brown Turkey The most dependable and easiest to grow, with purple-brown fruit.

Brunswick Earlier, and the fruits are larger.

Negro Largo This is the largest indoor fig for a heated greenhouse. The flesh is pale, the juice rich and heavy; the skin a mysterious black.

White Marseilles Starts green and becomes golden, oozing with rich juicy flesh, but only moderate size. This like the above varieties, can also be grown outside in warm areas, or in pots which take their turn in and out of the greenhouse.

Golden Berry (Physalis peruviana edulis)

Sow	Plant	Position	Harvest from	Propa-gation	Temperatures Night min.	Day max.	Notes
Feb.–March.	March–April	in house floor or pot-grown for planting outside	July Aug.–Sept.	18°C (65°F)	7°C (45°F)	16°C (60°F)	Good alongside crops with similar temperature needs

Known also as Cape gooseberry, this is a greatly improved form and will be completely new as a fruit to most home growers, who will be more familiar with the decorative, non-edible member of the Physalis family to which the golden berry belongs, the Chinese lantern. Happily, however, the golden berry does not inherit their anti-social ways of romping through flower borders, collapsing onto neighbours above ground, and using foul footwork down below with which nothing can compete. The golden berry is in a class all on its own. It has an indescribably exotic flavour. There are no pips or stones . . . you eat the lot, skin and all.

Very easy to grow, from seed to fruit in about 4 months, the golden berry continues cropping from year to year; it takes up no more space than a tomato plant. If you put it outside to grow after raising it in the greenhouse, it needs no protection from birds. The paper-thin Chinese lantern casing in which the berries form and ripen (*see drawing 27*) protects them from everything, including insects and children . . . unless they know what is hiding inside.

Growing

The golden berry can be cultivated entirely in a greenhouse, or grown outside until frost cuts it down. In mild areas with well drained soil it can remain outdoors all winter after the shoots are cut off, but even with straw protecting the roots, it is risky. Better to put it in a pot, keep it in

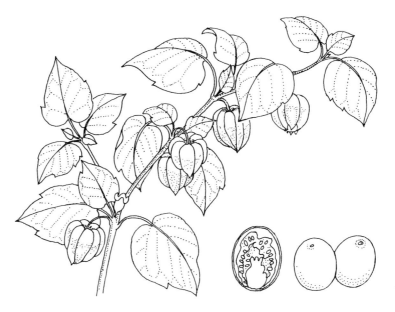

27

leaf, and give it an early start the following spring. Sow the seeds Feb–March in boxes or pots in a temperature of 18°C (65°F) in a soilless compost. As soon as they are large enough to handle transplant the seedlings singly to 12–15 cm (5–6 in) pots filled with a light but not rich compost. They produce too much leaf rather than fruit if pampered with good soil. Set the pots in the sunniest part of the greenhouse and move them further apart as they start to bush out. Or they can go into the borders; the shoots can be trained on to sticks or wires, in any way you would use for tomatoes. They are sturdy enough to need no supports whatever and will form fine bushes if you take off the main growing shoots when the plants are 30 cm (1 ft) high. They are not climbers or trailers, and it is up to you to keep them under control. Their eventual height is 0·90–1·20 m (3–4 ft).

Harvesting
The fruit starts to ripen about 75 days after sowing, depending on conditions. Test by gently parting the tip of a lantern and taking a look . . . the fruit should be golden rather than yellow and about the size of a dessert gooseberry. They are the easiest and least messy of all fruit to harvest. They are wonderfully juicy and sweet, but at the same time firm and if picked in their lanterns will stay fresh in the house far longer than other soft fruit.

Eat them as dessert just as you would raspberries or strawberries, or you can cook or freeze them. The flavour is unique.

Grapes

Sow	Plant	Position	Harvest from	Propa-gation	Temperatures Night min.	Day max.	Notes
	start into growth early Feb.	planted in floor of house or with roots outside house	late July on, according to variety	18°C (65°F)	10°C (50°F) 13°C (58°F) if heated	18°C (65°F)	Can cast dense shade but growing conditions suit most crops. Use space under vines for propagation early in the year before leaves fully expanded.

Grapes are one of the easiest fruits to grow, and many varieties do not need the high temperature some gardeners associate with them. Although an even temperature of 18°C (65°F) during flowering gives the best results, this is not necessary. The vines themselves are absolutely hardy and suitable varieties obligingly produce wine grapes in most uncomfortable situations. The dessert grape flourishes in a conservatory atmosphere . . . and takes more time about it. Some need a longer season than others to ripen.

The most likely problem is that grapes could completely crowd out everything else. Mature vines produce a dense canopy of foliage under which few plants will thrive. In a small greenhouse the vines must be strictly controlled, as you see them in wine-producing countries where they are pruned back every year. Never attempt to grow a vine in the border soil of a greenhouse which is less than 6 m (20 ft) long.

Method of growing

Where space is limited, vines can be grown in tubs or plastic pots (*see drawings 28 and 29*) about 30–35 cm (12–14 in), and will live up to 12 years and produce about 3·5 kg (8 lb) of grapes each year after careful pruning. Border grown plants, with their free-spreading roots live almost indefinitely, and produce a heavier crop. The border can be *inside* or *outside* the greenhouse. As the roots take up a large area, they are better planted outside a small greenhouse, and the top of the plant grown inside the glass. This gives the roots the benefit of rainwater. Plant them at the end or side of the greenhouse, whichever is more convenient, and lead the stems through holes in the wall just above soil level. If you are growing more than one, plant at least 0·90 m (3 ft) apart.

It is important not to allow the roots unlimited rooting space as this will encourage over-vigorous growth. Some restriction can be given if the roots are grown within the house where the base is of brick with a good foundation.

In borders Vine plants (usually called rods) are grown in pots until they are 2 or 3 years old and can be put into the borders. The soil must be

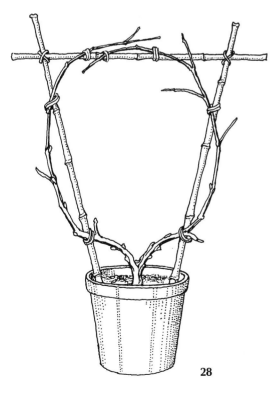

28

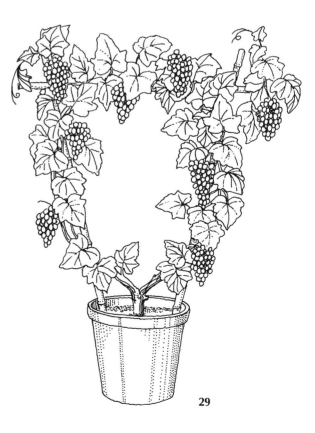

29

carefully prepared for the greedy, long-living roots. Good drainage is essential and if there is any doubt about this dig well down, keeping the topsoil in a separate heap. Put a layer of rubble or broken crocks at the base, about 60 cm (2 ft) deep. The ideal filling for this excavated trench-border is rotted turves mixed with a little grit and plenty of coarse bone meal, plus your top soil. Gardeners of country houses used to put a sheep carcass at the bottom, and each year, remove some of the top soil and add a garnish of a rabbit or hare. Should you be content with your existing soil, just add bonemeal and sulphate of potash, but the vines are not likely to outlive you as they did the 'old time' gardener.

Plant the vines when they are dormant in late winter, from February to early March, in a temperature of about 10°C (50°F) just before the roots start into action again. They must never be put in with their roots in the tight ball they have formed in the pots. Gently tease them out of their tangle, and spread them out, covering with about 5 cm (2 in) of soil.

In containers These can be plastic, wood, clay or anything which can provide good drainage and are at least 30 cm (12 in) across and 35 cm (14 in) deep. Put crocks in the bottom, and use the border mixture, John Innes Potting Compost No 3, or any commercial compost specially recommended for vines. They need a change of soil, but not of home, each year after pruning. Scrape away some of the old soil, and return the plant to the same pot, well cleaned, or to one of the same size filled with new compost, firmed well with hands or a rammer.

Pruning
This can be made to sound daunting but is easy once you get the hang of it and in a small greenhouse you must be ruthless it you want a good crop – the vine will recover rapidly. Grapes flower and form on the new growth made each year.

Establishing the vine Build up the main stem by selecting shoots at 50 cm (18 in) intervals along its length on alternate sides, rubbing out the rest. After the first season of growth cut back the length of rod by almost half to well-ripened wood. In the second season repeat this process, again selecting shoots which will form the future fruiting spurs. In the following winter again prune back the leading shoot and repeat this every year until the vine has reached the full extent of available space.

Pruning an established vine In December when the vines are dormant, and there is no danger of the cut shoots bleeding, prune every side shoot, almost back to main stem (rod), leaving two plump buds (eyes) to produce fruiting shoots (see *drawing 30*). When these start to grow, rub out the weaker, leaving just one shoot which is tied to wires as it develops. To prevent a tangled mass of new growth, pinch out the tips two leaves beyond the baby fruit (see *drawing 31*) or even while it is still in flower. Pinch out secondary growth at one leaf and tendrils at all times. Trim off the main growing points when they reach the height or space you can spare them. It is up to you to keep them in their place.

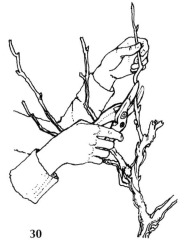

30

31

When the fruits start to swell thin them drastically, otherwise they will be small and misshapen. Start at the tip of each bunch and move upwards, taking out the smallest first. This may be done several times if you have been too timid with the first thinning and the grapes are nudging each other too closely. Use long pointed scissors and be careful not to handle the grapes or the bloom of their skin will be smudged. Tie up the shoulders of each bunch to the vines with soft string so there is room for the grapes to expand and give a good shape (*see drawing 32*).

Maintenance
Throughout the growing and fruiting season vines must be well watered and given balanced liquid feeds, particularly when the fruit starts to swell. Those in pots dry out quickly in summer and must be watched diligently. After the fruit is picked the pots can stand outside for the wood to ripen, watering until the leaves fall. In December return them to the greenhouse for pruning and re-potting. Support them in the most convenient way . . . against wires, or a framework of sturdy stakes or canes. They will need it only when the new growth starts in spring, until

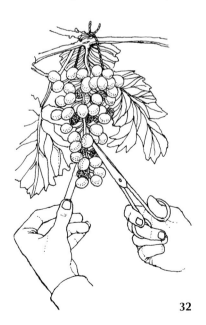

32

33

the fruit is picked, unlike the free-rooting ones. These border vines dry out less rapidly, particularly those with their feet out of doors, but still need a wary eye kept on them. Never be mingy with border watering, it has to go deeply to all the roots. A mulch of decayed manure or compost over the border will help retain the moisture. Those in containers can have a mulch of fresh potting compost, kept in place with a temporary raised collar of any stiff, but bendable, waterproof material, as though you were making a soufflé.

Propagation
Young vines will grow from the prunings you remove in winter. Make a bundle of the sturdiest and half bury them outside in soil. In February cut the shoots into short pieces, each with a single 'eye' or bud in the middle (*see drawing 33*). Slant the ends with a sharp knife. Lay the pieces flat on top of sandy soil in 7·5 cm (3 in) pots with the eyes uppermost. Add just enough soil to keep them anchored but not completely covered. Give them a temperature of 18°C (65°F), and in about six weeks new growth will appear from each bud, and roots start to develop. In summer put them in the greenhouse border, or 15 cm (6 in) pots, and the following winter re-pot into 25 cm (10 in) pots if they are not to remain in the border. They make welcome presents if you have a surplus.

Hazards
Pests which may attack vines usually have an appetite for young tender growth. They include *aphids, mealy bugs, red spider mites* and *scale insects*. These can be kept at bay by spraying with malathion as soon as the new shoots appear early in the year . . . don't wait till you can see the enemy because damage will already have been done. If *mildew* affects the plants use a dinocap spray after the flowers have set.

Recommended varieties
Black Hamburgh For a small unheated greenhouse.

Buckland Sweetwater (white) As above. There are many other varieties, including the delectable **Muscats**, if you can give them their exacting and costly requirements as regards heating.

Melons

Sow	Plant	Position	Harvest from	Propa- gation	Temperatures Night min.	Day max.	Notes
late Feb.	late Mar.	beds on house floor	July–Sept.	21°C (70°F)	16°C (60°F)	24°C (78°F)	Requirements are similar to those for cucumber.
March	April	beds on house floor	September		as above		

The flavour of a home grown melon is beyond price because it cannot be bought. Melons need almost the same treatment as cucumbers – (see page 27) with one important difference. After the early stages of growth they like a much drier atmosphere; a sunbath rather than a semi-sauna. Their greed for space in which to produce even a modest crop may rule them out for a small greenhouse, particularly if you are also growing cucumbers. But one or the other could always continue life outside, once they are raised, in a frame (*see drawing 34*), cloche or an open sunny protected spot.

Methods of growing

Sow the seed on edge in seed compost in 7·5 cm (3 in) pots during February and March in a moist atmosphere of 21°C (70°F). When the seedlings have 4–6 leaves and are 15–20 cm (6–8 in) tall they are ready to plant out, in the greenhouse, frame, cloches or, in the south, a warm sunny position. The soil must be well dug incorporating rotted manure or potting compost. Set them 60 cm (2 ft) apart on mounds (*see drawing 35*) making sure the soil ball top is just above the mound. In a greenhouse two plants will occupy a 1–1·20 m (3–4 ft) run of the border and produce, with luck, eight melons.

Maintenance

To be the proud owner of a good melon crop, you must never let them get thirsty, but do not water close to the stems or let any collect around

34

35

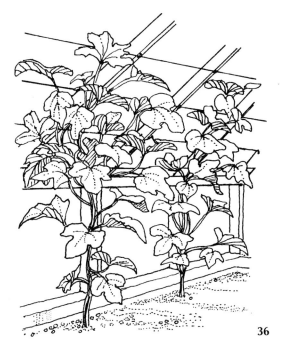

36

them as they are prone to 'collar rot'. This watering accompanied by regular feeding is essential until the fruits start to ripen, and must then be reduced to a trickle; otherwise the fruit will split. You can tell the moment to stop this 'spoon-feeding' when their unique aroma starts escaping from the skin.

Support and training

The plants can be trained on wires (*see drawing 36*) or a simple framework to fit the space available. Any plant which trails can go sideways and down, even more easily than up. So if your greenhouse arrangements allow it, the melons can recline horizontally on the floor or staging and will need no support. Let the main stem grow until it is 1–1·20 m (3–4 ft) high, or long, or reaches the top of the greenhouse, then pinch out the growing point. The side shoots produce the flowers and fruit. Pinch out these 'laterals' when they have produced about 6 leaves, so that other fruit-bearing side shoots will be encouraged to form. There is no strict rule about training plants, so do whatever suits you – and them – most comfortably. As the fruits get heavier, give them an undercarriage of netting such as a string or nylon bag, tied to an upper support (*see drawing 37*).

Pollination

In contrast to cucumbers, it is vital for the female flowers to be fertilized by male pollen. Wait till all the female flowers on one plant are open together on the same day, (they have a small swelling embryo fruit behind the flower.) Strip the petals from the male flower, break it off and stroke the stamens inside the female flowers (*see drawing 38*). Alternatively this can be done with a soft paint brush. It is important to choose a time of day when the pollen is dry, usually about noon. When

37

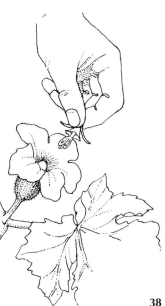

38

the little melons start to swell, allow only up to four of the best to develop, and remove all surplus fruitlets and shoots, so they will not rob the chosen ones. Only a really well grown, prolific plant will produce four fine melons. You may be well pleased with just two.

Harvesting

The ripe fruit of the melon gives off an unforgettable scent in the greenhouse which you will never get from bought imported ones because they could not travel in a mature condition. Apart from the scent, you can judge when the fruit is ripe when the top (flower end) relaxes when pressed gently.

Recommended varieties

Personal taste has to decide which you choose . . . between soft and hard flesh, coloured cream, white, green, pink or orange . . . and the flavour that goes with them.

Big-Ogen (greenhouse or cloche.) Round, early, delectable fruit with green-striped smooth yellowish skin and pale flesh. A compact space-saving bush.

Cantaloupe, Dutch Net (greenhouse, frame, cloche) Orange flesh with a beautiful flavour and quality which distinguishes this type of melon . . . quite different in texture from the firmer honeydew and ogen varieties, and well worth trying.

Golden Crispy (greenhouse.) An entirely edible cantaloupe – there is no noticeable skin. Oval with a creamy flesh, sweet and juicy, it is very vigorous and produces about 10 fruits on each plant weighing up to 1 lb each.

Ha-Ogen (Mini). The original Israeli strain, smaller than its part offspring above, but an even richer and sweeter, scented flavour. Each vine will produce about 10 melons, the size of a small grapefruit. Harvest from late July to late September.

Honey Drip (greenhouse) The finest flavour of all for most tastes, and very sweet. It puts honeydew, which it replaces, quite in the shade, being earlier and easier to grow.

Sweetheart (greenhouse or cloche.) Smooth pale green fruit with salmon pink sweet flesh. About 11 cm (4½ in) across.

Hazards

Basal stem rot The leaves droop and the stem rots at soil level. Caused by faulty planting and watering. The plants should be set on small mounds so that the soil around the base is kept dry and water cannot form puddles around the stem. Try not to splash the stems either.

Any other troubles will be the same as those of cucumbers.

Peaches and Nectarines

Sow	Plant	Position	Harvest from	Propa-gation	Temperatures Night min.	Day max.	Notes
	start into growth early Jan.	floor of house	July		7°C (45°F)	18°C (65°F)	Compatible crops are tomato and vegetable plants.
	late Feb.	floor of house	September		(unheated)	18°C (65°F)	

These are among the most delicious home-grown greenhouse crops. Bought peaches are nearly always expensive and compared with a fully ripe fruit eaten direct from the tree have the texture of, and just about as much flavour as, a turnip. The nectarine is a fuzz-less variety of peach, more reluctant to grow in the open or as bushes, but to many people, even more delectable. For their cultivation in a cold or heated greenhouse they should be treated in precisely the same way as peaches.

Planting

A lean-to greenhouse with a ready-made wall to train them against, is the easiest place (*see drawing 39*). An unheated or cool house suits them best, so choose the coldest position possible if the tree is to share it with plants which need rather warm conditions in winter, while the peach is resting. More than modest winter heat – about 5°C (41°F) can lure it into premature growth, resulting in bud-drop. The tree likes to start into growth in early spring in an unheated house. Fan trained two or three year olds can be bought from nurseries, grafted on to a rootstock.

39

A peach grown from the stone of one you enjoyed eating will seldom bear any resemblance to the original and is best treated just as a fun foliage pot plant.

Ask the nurseryman for a plant with a rootstock suitable for the space you can give the mature tree in your greenhouse. The best time to plant is in autumn. The soil should be reasonably rich and it is vitally important for it to be well drained. Dig out the existing border soil, to a depth of about 60 cm (2 ft) and strew a 10 cm (4 in) layer of broken bricks and flower pots on the bottom. The soil is less important than the drainage but needs a reasonable lime content in otherwise ordinary soil. It can contain well-decayed manure, loam and coarse bonemeal. Put in the tree at least 15–22 cm (6–9 in) away from the wall with the stem sloping towards the wall. Plant firmly to the same depth it was in the nursery or garden centre, which will be shown by the soil mark on the stem.

Pruning and training

The fruit grows on shoots made during the previous year, and it is utterly irresponsible to approach any pruning until you recognize the difference between the two kinds of buds, or you will have all leaf and no fruit. The *round* ones will bear the fruit and the *pointed* ones the growing shoots. Pure fruit buds will never produce any wood growth and it is useless to cut back to one if a shoot is needed to fill a gap or expand the growth. However, when the buds form in triplets, it is quite safe to cut back to just above them, as two will be blossom (fruit) buds and the third a wood bud.

All stone fruits object to severe pruning, both under glass or in the open, and must be given enough space so that this is not necessary. The less pruning the better, for the tree and crop. The aim must be to cover the wall space with branches coming low down from the trunk in a fan shape, so each branch can get the most sun and air to ripen it. A sappy, sallow shoot will never produce fruit fit to eat.

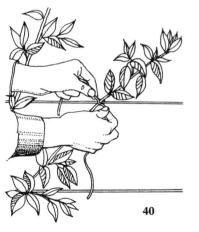

A bought two or three year old, fan-trained plant will have a number of side branches. If there is still a central stem, this should be cut out when the side branches are about 50 cm (18 in) long. If allowed to remain, your plant would turn into a tree, and the fruit-bearing side branches languish from lack of nourishment which will go to sustain the sparsely bearing main stem. Tie the branches to horizontal wires close to the angle from which they emerge from the main stem (*see drawing 40*). Snip off the ends to a single wood-bud, to keep the sap flowing.

40

As the young shoots develop in spring, the fan shape is kept in control by dis-budding. Ruthlessly rub out any shoots going in the wrong direction, as soon as you see them, so the tree does not waste effort on unwanted wood. The unwanted buds grow behind and in front of the main branches (*see drawing 41*). It can almost be done with the eyes shut, just rubbing with the fingers. The remaining side-growing ones should be thinned to about 30 cm (12 in) apart to produce plenty of fruiting branches the following year.

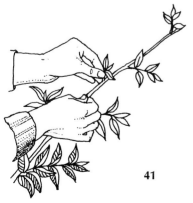

41

Autumn or winter pruning is simply a matter of cutting out the old wood which has just carried the fruit, replacing it by a shoot produced in the current season from a bud near the base of the fruiting shoot.

Pollination

Peaches and nectarines need a little help in this matter when grown under glass. Flowers should form in February and March, depending on the greenhouse temperature. Use a soft paintbrush, a rabbit tail or piece of cotton wool tied to a bamboo cane, and just touch the flowers to transfer the pollen from stamens to stigma. Do this daily, about midday when the pollen is dry and the tree is in flower, because the pollen does not all ripen at the same time.

Fruit thinning

More fruit will often set than the tree has the strength to bring up properly. Don't be hasty at removing the baby fruits, wait till they are the size of small walnuts. Where they are in pairs, take off the weaker one and the final thinning should leave a fruit about every 25 cm (10 in) apart on the branch. These will be most succulent and special. For quantity rather than quality, thin less ruthlessly.

Water and food

In its early life the tree must not be gorged or it would make too much leaf growth, but once it has started to bear fruit, the border should have a dressing of potting compost in winter, and a general purpose fertilizer in spring. The roots need large quantities of water frequently when they are in leaf.

Hazards

The worst torment is *leaf curl*, which, if allowed to continue over the years will kill the tree. The leaves curl up, thicken and turn red. All you can do at first is to remove and burn all the infected leaves and twigs. The most likely pests are *aphids* (the leaves curl up without thickening) and *red spider*, which makes the leaves look dry and shrivelled and can spoil the crop. A disease called *dieback* speaks for itself. The tip of a shoot dies and the rest of it follows suit.

Remedy The year following attack by leaf curl spray with Bordeaux mixture just before flower and leaf buds open. To control aphis spray with derris or a systemic insecticide like dimethoate. For red spider, see *Pests and diseases*. Dieback can be checked in spring by pruning back to a shoot or bud where there is no brown stain in the cut wood.

Recommended varieties

Very much a matter of personal taste, usually between white or yellow flesh.

PEACHES
Duke of York Has large, yellow-fleshed fruit; ripens in July.

Hale's Early Ripens in July the white flesh is melting and delicious if you want your delicacies small and refined rather than robust.

Peregrine The most reliable and generally popular peach for both indoors and out, though not for the epicure. It has a highly coloured skin and white flesh, is self-fertile and starts ripening from early August in an unheated house and earlier where there is heat.

NECTARINES

Early Rivers This variety is ripe by early August; a large, light yellow fruit flushed with brilliant crimson, and rich-flavoured greenish-white flesh. Try and find a nursery where you can buy and taste the fruit before you buy its parent!

Pineapple For nectarines this variety has everything in its favour – a rich orange and crimson fruit with delicious yellow flesh which ripens in early September.

Sadly, peaches and nectarines eventually need a good deal of space. A fully mature fan-trained tree will grow to stretch over the wall of a 5·5 m (18 ft) lean-to greenhouse.

Strawberries

Sow	Plant	Position	Harvest from	Propa-gation	Temperatures Night min.	Day max.	Notes
	plant August house mid Jan.–early Feb.	on shelves near glass	late April–early May		5°C (40°F)	16°C (60°F)	Raise the temperature gradually after housing to a minimum of 10°C (50°F) Grow alongside vegetable plants, fig

42

Home grown strawberries in time for Christmas is the ambition of many otherwise modest greenhouse owners – perhaps more for the prestige than the flavour. But it really should be left to the professional who can use all the tricks of frosting the plants at the right moment, coddling them and giving them artificial light. The amateur can be well pleased to be picking them by the end of April, about a month before those grown outdoors. Strawberries are easy to grow in pots and need greenhouse space for only a few months.

Method of growing

Buy pot-grown runners and plant up in late August. Otherwise choose healthy young runners from maiden (one-year-old) plants. Remove the blossom from the parent (see *drawing 42*) so it will produce strong runners. In late June or early July, peg down the runner plantlets with

43

bent wire into small pots of light soil sunk into the ground around the mother plant (*see drawing 43*). Take no more than six from each. The maiden 'parent' is left in the ground to fruit the following year. Once the runner roots have filled their pots, cut them adrift from their parents (*see drawing 44*) stand them closely in semi-shade and keep well watered.

Towards the end of August re-pot them into bigger ones, 15–17 cm (6–7 in). Put drainage crocks in the bottom and fill with John Innes No 3 potting compost. When tipping out of the small pots, gently crack the crusty surface of the root ball so that they can breathe and take in their new nourishment more easily. Plant towards the side of the pot rather than in the centre, with the tops of the clumps (crowns) just clear of the surface, which should be about 1 cm (½ in) below the rim. Stand the pots in semi-shade again to settle down, on a path or natural floor, water moderately but don't allow them to dry out.

After about two weeks transfer them to a sunny, well-ventilated place . . . if possible a cold frame, until mid-January. Give them plenty of air and protect them only from severe frosts or real deluges of rain. When the greenhouse temperature is at least 4°C (40°F) and not above 10°C (50°F) at night and a little warmer by day bring in a few pots at a time to start into more rapid growth, to have a continuous supply rather than a sudden glut. Bring in the follow-ups when the first batch is in flower and follow the same routine with the rest.

Pollination

Most strawberries are self-fertile, but there will be no pollinating insects about when they start to flower so touch the flowers with cotton wool tied to the end of a cane so that pollination is certain. From the moment the fruits form, give the plants a weekly feed. Perfectionists thin out the fruit once it has set leaving no more than 6–8 berries on a plant. But for family eating, when big is not necessarily best, don't bother. As the fruit colours give it as much ventilation as possible, without upsetting the other inmates of the greenhouse.

Protection and support

The berries must be kept clean and clear of the pots and compost. This

44

45

will depend on the variety and the position they are growing in. A high shelf will give them all possible light (*see drawing 45*) and the berries can trail happily downwards. Pots sunk into border soil need straw under them (*see drawing 46*) or to be tied to stakes or wire with raffia. Some need only forked twigs to give them a lift, and some newer varieties are self-supporting. Re-plant them out of doors to recover immediately after fruiting.

Hazards
Outdoor strawberries are the victims of large gangs of pests and diseases, from which the 'forced' ones are happily protected, if they are healthy to begin with. If any do fall sick, don't bother with a cure. Throw them out, clean up their surroundings and start again. Misshapen fruits are due to faulty pollination so this job should be done more thoroughly next year if this problem occurs.

Recommended varieties
Buy only virus-free plants from growers or garden centres with a Ministry certificate of health. Propagate your own runners only for the first year after buying uncertified stock, then replace with new stock. The old 'mother' plants can be kept for fruit production but new mother plants should be grown as far away as possible from fruiting plants to reduce the risk of spread of disease.

Cambridge Prizewinner Early, large fruit, of good flavour.

46 **Gorella** The best of all for forcing. A second-early, large and good cropper.

49

PERPETUAL-FRUITING OR REMONTANT STRAWBERRIES

These fruit almost continuously from July till the first frosts. The fruits are not as large as the normal varieties and they form long-lasting compact bushes. Grow them in containers such as tower pots, or those with protruding lips round them, and move them into the greenhouse in late autumn to continue fruiting. Make sure they are light enough to be mobile when filled with drainage material and compost. Remove all the flowers early in the season to concentrate fruiting later in the year. They do not usually produce many runners, but any which do form should be left on to increase the crop.

Recommended varieties

Gento Produces large, excellently flavoured fruit; a heavy cropper.

Rabunda Heavy crop of bright, regular shaped fruits.

Trellisa Unusual. Flowers and fruits freely on its runners, which, as the name implies can be trained against trellis, wires or rigid netting.

A Few 'Fun' Fruit

Not to be taken too seriously as a contribution to the family table, here are a few exotic strangers that are interesting to grow, have decorative foliage and will, with a bit of luck, produce edible fruit. Some, like the Citrus mini-orange have even the bonus of flowers that are sweetly scented. Seeds are obtainable from specialist firms such as Thompson and Morgan of Ipswich.

Citrus Mini-orange (Calamondin mitis)

Sow	Plant	Position	Harvest from	Propa-gation	Temperatures Night min.	Day max.	Notes
Feb./March	April–May	light and airy	following season	24°C (75°F)	5°C (40°F)	21°C (70°F)	Scented white flowers, attractive foliage

These are pot-grown plants which require to be kept frost-free throughout the winter. According to the conditions which they are given, they may start producing fruit from the age of about 18 months from seed-sowing. The fruit is more suitable for flavouring and colouring use, particularly for jams and sauces, rather than producing oranges which can be eaten fresh (see drawing 47).

47

Method of growing

Seeds should be sown in a proprietary compost and just covered with a sifting of compost before firming. Keep at a temperature of 24°C (75°F) until after germination. When the seedlings are at the right stage to be handled they should be carefully transplanted into individual pots of about 7·5 cm (3 in) diameter and need to be grown on then under warm and humid conditions, but shaded from direct sunlight. Depending on growing conditions, the plants can be ready to move out of the small pots into larger 25–30 cm (10–12 in) diameter pots after about 3 months.

Watering

It is advantageous if the pots can be watered upwards from the bottom by standing them in a saucer of water. This also produces the correct degree of humidity which is desirable for best results. As the plants grow they should be given supports and placed in a light warm position, although during the summer they can be moved outdoors to a warm position with some shelter. Watering is eased if the plants are plunged to the rim of their pots in the border. Spraying, as recommended for Guava, aids fruit bearing.

Overwintering

Citrus mini-oranges should be brought inside again well before there is any risk of frost and because they are not hardy should then be kept at a temperature of 5°C (40°F) throughout the winter. When flowering begins, up to 18 months after seed-sowing, they should be syringed along with the foliage to encourage pollination and to keep the right conditions to grow well up to the stage when the fruit is formed. One of the attractive features of the plant is that the flowers are white and scented and decorative.

Dwarf Banana (Musa)

Sow	Plant	Position	Harvest from	Propa-gation	Temperatures Night min.	Day max.	Notes
April	June	pots – may be put outside during summer	12–18 months after seed-sowing according to temp. and given winter heat	21°C (70°F)	7°C (45°F)	15°C (60°F)	Needs humid conditions like other exotic plants

The most appealing, rapid growing pot plant from seed, it will, in obliging conditions, produce edible fruit. Not the large imported ones, but finger-sized, probably with seeds in them (*see drawing 48*). It takes only about three months from seed to become a really respectable sized plant which

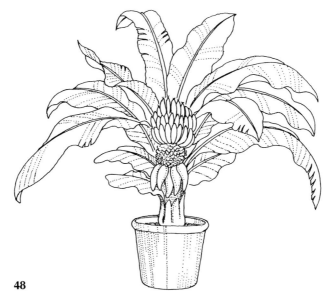

48

will grow extremely large, given sufficient root space. In nine months you can be housing a youngster some 1·50 × 1·50 m (5 × 5 ft). However, to be rewarded with edible fruit, the plant must be kept growing strongly throughout the winter with a fairly humid atmosphere, and this is not easy to achieve.

Method of growing
Put the large black seeds into a small container and pour near-boiling water over them. Leave to cool and continue soaking in warm water for up to 72 hours. Put them into a seed compost and keep in deep shade at a temperature of about 21°C (70°F). When the seedlings can be handled, transfer them to 12·5 cm (5 in) pots. As they continue over the next 8 months transfer them to potting compost and finally into 20–30 cm (8–12 in) pots. Water well in summer and reduce it to a minimum during winter.

Temperature requirements Try and keep a temperature of about 15°C (60°F) during the day and not let it fall below 7°C (45°F) at night. To produce bananas within 10 months from sowing, the ideal temperature is 21°C (70°F). For more patient growers with less exotic conditions, the fruit takes about 18 months in the semi-luxury of 15°C (60°F). If practicable, put the plants outside during the warm months when the night temperature is unlikely to drop below 7°C (45°F).

Guava, yellow (Psidium guajava)

Sow	Plant	Position	Harvest from	Temperatures			Notes
				Propa-gation	Night min.	Day max.	
To choice	To choice	Large pot	2 years after seed sowing	24°C (75°F)	−1°C (30°F)	18°C (65°F)	Likes humid conditions and some shade; grow alongside cucumber

Another 'fun' fruit, perhaps more valuable for its decorative foliage, but it can produce aromatic edible fruits in up to 2 years from seed-sowing. By comparison with the mini-orange, guavas are able to withstand perhaps 1 or 2°C (2°F or 3°F) of frost but you are more likely to achieve fruit if you do not allow the temperature to fall below 40°F (5°C). It also aids fruit production if you spray the flowers and foliage regularly from the time when the flower buds appear until the fruit forms.

Method of growing
The seed has a hard shell and before sowing it should be soaked in tepid water for 48 hours. Seeds should be sown singly in any proprietary compost and germinated at a temperature of 24°C (75°F). Again when the seedlings are large enough to handle they should be carefully moved to individual 7·5 cm (3 in) diameter pots and returned to a warm and humid atmosphere but given shade from direct sun. About 3 months later they can be moved to their final quarters into 25–30 cm (10–12 in) pots. The fruit has a pink flesh and is very juicy and distinctively flavoured; you can either eat it as dessert or it can be made into jam. The Yellow Guava grows to a height of 1·20–1·80 m (4–6 ft) and bears white flowers in June. (See drawing 49).

49

50

Passion Fruit (Granadilla)

| Sow | Plant | Position | Harvest from | Temperatures | | | Notes |
				Propagation	Night min.	Day max.	
To choice	April–May	pots	August	18°C (64°F)	5°C (40°F)	21°C (70°F)	Needs humid conditions; grow alongside cucumber

The family to which this belongs is characterized by very vigorous decorative tendril climbers and is not to be contemplated where space is limited. They are not fully hardy although many gardeners do manage to grow them on a south facing wall out of doors. The fanciful, complex blooms, of various irridescent shades, will not, in the case of most species, ripen into fruit; although *Passiflora caerulea*, normally grown for its flowers, will sometimes produce edible fruit after a hot summer. In general, however, they must have heat and great humidity to produce those golden-skinned, thirst-quenching delicacies, and this can only be achieved in a greenhouse. You must be prepared to spend a good deal of time training and restraining the growth and pay particular attention to their water and temperature requirements.

Method of growing
Be careful to buy seeds of the edible passion fruit as there are many varieties and those listed in flower catalogues may not be suitable. If you are hoping to grow fruit to eat, *P. edulis* is a good choice (*see drawing 50*). This has flowers with purple and white corona filaments and white petals, measuring up to 5 in (12·5 cm) across. The fruit are some 3 in (7·5 cm) in diameter and have firm yellow or purple skin and are aromatic. Suitable only for a large greenhouse is *P. quadrangularis*, an even more flamboyant plant, having reddish flowers measuring up to 7 in (17·5 cm)

across and yellowish green oval fruits reaching as much as 8 in (20 cm) in length. It takes its name from its square sectioned winged stems.

The seeds have hard outer shells, so to speed germination soak in tepid water for up to two days. To keep the water tepid stand it in an airing cupboard or any constantly warm place. You can sow at any time of year in a box or pot of seed compost. To germinate they need a temperature of 18°C (65°F).

When the seedlings are large enough to handle, transplant them carefully into individual 7·5 cm (3 in) pots. Keep them moist, and the atmosphere around them warm and humid but not in direct sun.

After about three months they will be ready to move to their permanent pots, 30–40 cm (12–15 in) across. This will automatically restrict the roots and encourage flowering. Use fibrous loam with sand and lots of peat. Passion fruit plants must be kept from making merry in the border of a greenhouse by severely disciplining their roots. The best way to water is from the bottom. Stand the pot in a container and let the roots suck it up. Water freely in the summer and keep fairly dry in winter. Give them somewhere to climb and in two or three years they will fruit really well. Some plants fruit within 18–30 months, depending on variety and when sown. The most important points to watch, in order to get fruit are that the temperature must not drop below 5°C (40°F); that they need spraying, both flowers and foliage, to keep the atmosphere humid; and that they need a light airy position.

Both species need to be hand pollinated with a small camel hair brush.

Pruning In winter to within two buds of the old wood. Remove weak shoots completely in spring.

Vegetables for the Gourmet

Producing top-quality vegetables for your family is a good enough reason in itself for investing in a greenhouse – whether you decide to stick to those basic standbys for the salad bowl, lettuce, cucumber or tomatoes, or try your hand at sweet peppers, aubergines or early potatoes, delicacies that seldom, if ever, seem to come down in price.

Aubergines (Eggplant)

Sow	Plant	Position	Harvest from	Temperatures Propa-gation	Night min.	Day max.	Notes
early Mar.	mid-April	floor of house or 15 cm (6 in) pots 60 cm (2 ft) apart	July	24°C (75°F)	16°C (60°F)	21°C (70°F)	Compatible with tomatoes and peppers

Though semi-tropical, aubergines will mature outside if given a nursery upbringing, but they have a much better rate of success if reared in the greenhouse.

The fruits vary in shape from egg-shaped to oblong to sausage shaped, and in colour from purple to white, according to variety.

Method of growing
Sow the seed singly into 6·5 cm (2½ in) peat pots in a temperature of about 24°C (75°F) in March. When the seedlings are about 7 cm (3 in) high, transplant them into 15 cm (6 in) pots or even larger ones. Let them stay in a really warm position and harvest when the fruits are a full colour (see drawing 51). If left on the plant too long they become hard and dry.

Recommended varieties
Long Tom Glossy purple-black fruit about 17 cm (7 in) long and 3·5 cm (1½ in) in diameter. This variety is a tremendous cropper and will produce 40–50 fruits if they are picked young and not allowed to mature on the plant and exhaust it.

Short Tom Prolific producer of fruit about 12·5 cm (5 in) long and 5 cm (2 in) thick.

Slim Jim Long, light purple fruits set in clusters of 3–5, with attractive violet foliage. Matures early.

51

Beans, French

Sow	Plant	Position	Harvest from	Temperatures Propagation	Temperatures Night min.	Temperatures Day max.	Notes
End Feb.	early April	In border or pots	May	18°C (65°F)	13°C (55°F)	21°C (70°F)	A few plants at the end of a house can give a useful early crop; grow alongside cucumber
End Mar.	May (outdoors)		July	18°C (65°F)			

Dwarf or bush French beans

These are among the most prized summer vegetables and particularly suitable for a greenhouse. They have the advantage over those grown outside, being much earlier and easier to pick (*see drawing 52*). The pots can be put on staging at any height to suit your back. Being clear of the soil, the pods do not get rain-splashed or nibbled by slugs.

Methods of growing

There are several ways. Choose the one which suits you best.

1 In February sow the seeds individually in 7·5 cm (3 in) pots of seed compost, and when large enough to handle, transfer to 15 cm (6 in) pots filled with potting compost. They can stay in these or go into the greenhouse border.

2 Sow the seeds 4 or 5 to a 20 cm (8 in) pot or 5 or 6 to 25 cm (10 in) pot. Half fill the pots with John Innes compost No 2 and add more compost when the plants are about 15 cm (6 in) high.

3 To raise plants which are to grow in the open in May and June, sow the seed in March, harden them off, and plant out when all danger of frost is over.

52

53

Keep the compost moist and give plenty of ventilation in warm weather. To help the flowers to set into beans, spray the plants daily when the weather is warm and sunny. Keep picking the beans from the moment they are finger-length (the choice of finger is yours), so the plant will keep producing more. If left to swell the plant will concentrate on ripening seed and stop flowering, and the pods themselves will not be fit for cooking.

Recommended varieties
Remus The pods form above the foliage which gives them more air and light to grow quickly. It makes them easier to pick and stay clean if to be set outside.

Royal Burgundy This has succulent purple pods which turn green in cooking. Also recommended: **The Prince; Gitana; Gold Crop**, which has shiny yellow pods.

Climbing French beans
The runner bean is not suitable for indoor production although early plants can be raised under glass for planting out of doors once the risk of frost is passed. Climbing French beans take up a good deal of space in a greenhouse and are best suited for the lean-to type with an expanse of

south-facing wall. They are sown in the same manner and left in pots or put 30 cm (1 ft) apart in the greenhouse border. Train them up to the roof up taut string, wire or canes, twisting the plants around the support in a similar manner to that recommended for tomatoes (*see drawing 53*). Given warm conditions with frequent spraying with water and generous ventilation on sunny days they should grow vigorously and crop well. A single plant at the end of a greenhouse should provide quite a useful crop over a longer period than the dwarf French bean can give. Do not sow the plant too early as under cool conditions it is not easy to pollinate and then cropping suffers.

Recommended variety
Blue Lake Stringless green pods.

Hazards
The plants are subject to attacks by glasshouse *red spider* but the best control for this is frequent damping down.

Courgette, Marrow, Squash

Sow	Plant	Position	Harvest from	Propa-gation	Night min.	Day max.	Notes
					Temperatures		
late April	end of May (outdoors)	In good light while indoors	July	16°C (60°F)	10°C (50°F)	21°C (70°F)	Harden off before planting outdoors

Although these vary widely in shape, size, colour and growing habit – some bush and some trailing – they all belong to the same family, which in Britain we call 'vegetable marrow' and in America, 'squash'. The pumpkin also belongs to this large family. The much-prized courgette – known as 'zucchini' in America, just to make matters more complicated – is simply the dwarf or immature version of the vegetable marrow. Fortunately despite the confusion of naming, all the members of this family have similar needs and to simplify things they are referred to here as marrows.

Method of growing
The plants are tender, and a greenhouse gives them an early and secure start, and where there is enough space, the whole season under glass. When raising plants which are later to go in the open, you can choose any variety which suits your taste, but for permanent summer residence choose bush ones, not trailers. These can be trained to supports, allowed to sprawl on the floor or hang down from pots but they are too cumbersome for a small house and need too much attention with

stopping and pinching out runners to be worth the trouble. Though they fruit later outside they are perfectly happy in anything but a dire summer, meandering about willy-nilly and cropping until frost kills them.

Sowing

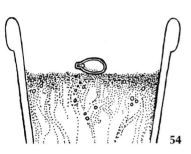

54

Plants of this family in general hate to have their roots disturbed from the moment they produce their first root. This is why many plants, sown in the open where they are to grow in May, frequently overtake and crop earlier than those put out after a greenhouse babyhood. They are often sturdier too if the indoor ones have not been properly grown and hardened off. Because of this root touchiness, the seeds are best sown individually into 5–7·5 cm (2–3 in) pots (preferably peat ones) filled with moist soilless compost. Put in the seeds on their sides rather than flat to prevent rotting (*see drawing 54*) leaving about 1 cm (½ in) of compost over them.

Sowing time must be geared to planting time and whether this is to be in the greenhouse frame, cloche or the open. Seeds take four or five weeks to produce a seedling ready to harden off for planting outside in late May and early June when frosts are over. So late April is a good time to sow these. Any to remain in the house in pots or the border can be sown a few weeks earlier.

Maintenance

Marrows must always be given a very rich soil and good drainage. . . . water freely at all times *around* the plants, *not* over them. When transplanting, take great care not to disturb the roots . . . the seedlings should not know they have changed homes. Once the marrows start to swell, give a weak liquid feed every 15 days.

Pollinating

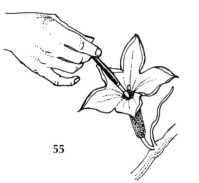

55

This procedure can safely be left to insects early in summer, but earlier in the year hand pollination is essential, particularly for those under glass; they will start to fruit much earlier and have heavier crops. This can be done with a soft paintbrush, dusting pollen from the male flowers on to that of the female. Or remove a male flower (this has no swelling behind the thin stem) on a dry day; fold back the petals and push gently into the female flower (*see drawings 55 and 56*).

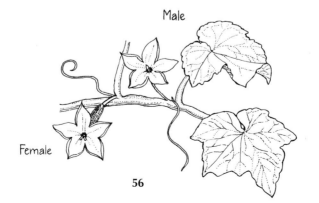

Male

Female

56

Harvesting

The courgette varieties in particular must be cut while still young and tender, *ie*, when only a few inches long and with the flower still attached to the end. Apart from the fact that they taste much better, this treatment encourages heavy cropping. Even one fruit allowed to grow into adolescence will send a message to the parent plant that it is reaching maturity and the parent will stop producing new flowers.

For varieties of vegetable marrow which are to be stored in the winter, allow the fruits to mature on the plant and remove before frosts. Store as for melons, in nets in a cool frostfree room or shed.

Recommended varieties

Bushes with compact habit which produce small fruits over a long period:

Baby Crookneck Compact, early with bright yellow fruits with bent necks. Best flavour of all, particularly when very young. Heavy crop.

Courgette Golden skinned or green.

Custard White Flattish with scalloped edges, delectable flavour, large crop.

Patty Pan Compact, enormous crop, picked when 7 cm (3 in) across, can be eaten raw in salad or lightly cooked.

Zucchini Golden skinned or green.

Trailing varieties

Vegetable Spaghetti The inside is scooped out and can be eaten like spaghetti (*see drawing 57*).

Little Gem Can be eaten at golf or tennis ball size, or left to grow larger for September–October eating. Can also be stored.

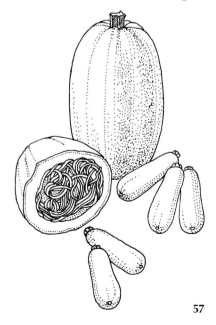

57

Endive

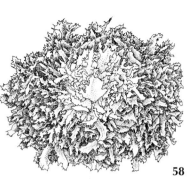

58

See table for chicory, except that seed is sown in July.

Endive is a salad vegetable which can be grown throughout its life outdoors or, for autumn and winter use, brought inside and blanched. It is like lettuce in texture, but needs to be blanched in order to get rid of the rather bitter flavour which the unblanched plants can have. Seed is sown in July, preferably in a sheltered sunny position or in a cold frame or under lights (*see drawing 58*).

Blanching

Plants are ready to be lifted for blanching when they are about 3 months old from sowing and the blanching consists of gathering the leaves together and tying them with raffia so that the light is excluded from the heart leaves. Plants can be lifted and brought inside for this purpose. Blanching takes up to 3 weeks in autumn and winter and a few plants should be brought inside from time to time in order to keep a succession going.

Recommended variety

Batavian Green For autumn and winter use.

Herbs, Annual

A particular joy of the greenhouse is being able to grow those short-lived tender herbs that can transform a simple dish into an experience for the gourmet. They are alas, rather half-hearted about our climate . . . mostly being natives of Mediterranean countries . . . and cannot be relied on to swell their foliage to the full, or even to survive, in a dull, wet summer. The ones which it is essential to make room for in a greenhouse are basil, chervil, dill and marjoram.

Method of growing

Tender annual herbs need very little space. They can be reared in the greenhouse in containers, spend summer outside, so leaving space for other things, and return home in autumn so you can keep cutting them till they expire, and a new batch of seedlings is ready for the cook. Your favourite, most tender and useful ones can stay permanently in the house, particularly in a temperamental summer. Those you put outside in their pots or containers must be in a sunny, sheltered position. They can rest on soil or hard standing (compacted ash or gravel), and if you sink the pots to their rims in the ground they will need less watering. Beware of feeding succulent herbs as this can encourage too much foliage and destroy much of the natural flavour.

Containers These can be anything from 15 cm (6 in) pots to larger ones, boxes, or anything which suits you. Annual herbs prefer a light, rather chalky soil to a heavy one. Use John Innes No 1 compost and have plenty of drainage holes covered with crocks, to keep the holes clear and the drainage free-flowing, as it would be in their native chalky Mediterranean hillsides. Sow the seed of annuals in the container in which you intend them to continue. Barely cover with compost and thin out the seedlings if too many germinate and crowd each other. Keep up a plentiful supply of new-sown seed, even if some of it is wasted, and you should be able to keep an everlasting crop. The most used herbs can go straight from the greenhouse to the kitchen windowsill, so there is no need even to go outside to add the finishing touch to a dish.

Sweet basil and bush basil

The whole plant has a spicy aroma that is released by the lightest touch. A pot of basil in an open window will keep away flies and other disagreeable insects.

Sweet basil is the more succulent but delicate of the two. It rarely stretches to the 60 cm (2 ft) height reached in its homelands, but the 5 cm (2 in) long leaves are full of rich flavour and should not be cooked, just chopped and sprinkled onto dishes, particularly those with tomato. Nip out the centres of the young plants so that they will not shoot up into leggy plants but instead branch out into a bushy shape.

Bush basil is less succulent and a miniature variety, no higher than 15–30 cm (6–12 in), more shrubby, with a thick mass of small leaves. Sweet basil is more productive and tastier, while bush basil is more adaptable for growing in pots . . . in the greenhouse, on balconies or window boxes (*see drawing 59*).

Chervil

A quick growing annual with feathery, light green leaves resembling parsley (*see drawing 60*) which it can replace when there is a lapse in its

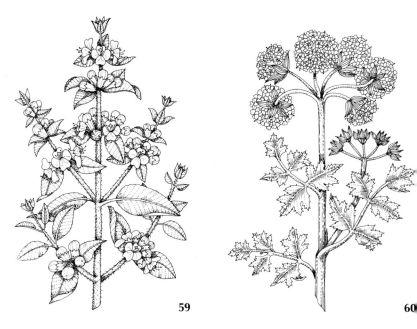

59   **60**

61

growing routine. Unlike parsley, the warm, spicy, slightly aniseed flavour of chervil is lost in cooking, and must be sprinkled only at the last moment onto egg dishes, salads, soups, fish sauces, to make their unusual impact. They are in particular harmony with buttered new potatoes, young carrots and baby broad beans.

Fresh seed is essential. Sow it frequently and in small quantities and keep it moist in semi-shade as it quickly goes to seed. If the leaves start to turn purple brown, this is not a disease but a warning signal that a young batch of plants will soon be needed, and they cannot go on much longer. Always pick the leaves from the outside of the cluster as you do parsley to keep the heart producing new ones. If a few flower heads are left to go to seed it can be used for a new sowing as soon as it is ripe, as it stays viable for only a short time. The pretty curled leaves form low-growing mats, taking up little space.

Dill

Enchanting in looks and flavour, this feather-leaved annual (*see drawing 61*) should be grown by anyone with a heart and nose for cooking. The plants grow from 45 cm–1 m (1½–3 ft) and look like a refined version of fennel. If in doubt, crushed dill leaves have a hint of caraway while fennel has an unmistakable aniseed scent. Both leaves and seeds are splendid cooking playthings. As with most of the annuals, the leaf flavour is lost if cooked long. The chopped leaves add mystery to sauces for fish and vegetables, soups, seafood, cheese and egg dishes, chicken and meat, as well as salads. The seed is indispensable in pickled cucumber, chutneys, crushed into apple pie, or cooked with vegetables which need very little water such as shredded cabbage or crushed onto cauliflower as it is being steamed.

After the seedling stage, dill does not grow well in pots. They can be transplanted to the open ground, to the border of the greenhouse, or

62

sown into large boxes in which they remain. They need sun and must not be irritated by draughts or strong winds. Sow the seed continuously from spring onwards for a constant supply. Leave a few flower heads to provide seed, pinch out the buds of the rest of the plants as soon as they appear. This treatment, combined with cutting the leaves for use will encourage well branched growth, rather than feathery upright poles.

Sweet (or knotted) marjoram

The most aromatic and versatile of all the marjorams, this must be treated as half-hardy in Britain. The flower buds which form during the summer and autumn on sturdy 30 cm (12 in) miniature bushes appear in clusters of pearly knots at regular intervals up the stem – hence its other name, 'knotted marjoram'. These modest buds and small leaves contain the quite unsuspected magic flavour of the plant. The herb is best in league with pork, beef, fowl, rabbit, stuffings and kebabs. The knotted buds should be cut on the stems and dried before they open.

There are dozens of different marjorams varying in hardiness and performance. All can be grown from seed in a light well-drained, slightly acid soil, and can be grown in pots and boxes big enough for their vigorous root systems. They must be kept in full sun. Bring in the plants to the greenhouse in the winter and sow new seed of those which seem to be failing (*see drawing 62*).

Lettuce

Sow	Plant	Position	Harvest from	Propagation	Temperatures Night min.	Day max.	Notes
Nov./Dec.	Dec./Jan.	In border, cloches or frame	March/April	13°C (55°F)	7°C (45°F)	16°C (60°F)	These crops can be grown without heat if required. Harvesting is then delayed by comparison with the heated crop early in the season.
January	February	As above	April/May	13°C (55°F)			
February	March	As above	May	13°C (55°F)			
February	March/April (outdoors)		May				
Mar./Jul.	April/Aug. outdoors		May/Oct.				

One of the easiest vegetables to grow, yet one of the most difficult to grow well at all seasons throughout the year. Modern methods of plant breeding have produced varieties for an assortment of conditions and tastes (*see drawing 63*). There are Butterhead and Crisp, both cabbage varieties; Cos varieties of many statures . . . miniature to immense and some self-curling; loose-leaf varieties, which are picked like spinach, a few leaves at a time, and never form a heart; 'short day' varieties which

flourish in the gloom of winter, and 'long day' ones which do best between May and June, when they get the most light and sun.

Seedlings can be raised to be planted outside from March onwards, and grown entirely indoors during the winter and autumn months, or longer if you can spare the space. To produce a perfect lettuce of any type, it must be sweet and fresh tasting, not just a wrapping or filling to make something dull, even duller. The perfect lettuce heart is a solo delicacy, merely dipped into melted butter between each bite. The only way to achieve this is to keep them growing fast and continuously from seed to finish, with no interruptions.

Method of growing
Sow regularly all through the year using a selection of varieties. Those which are being raised to crop outside must not be sown too early or their growth will be checked if they have to be put out before the soil has warmed, which tempts them into 'bolting' and running to seed prematurely. The soil must be rich and well-drained so the plants can mature quickly.

Sow seeds thinly in late autumn and spring in boxes or pots in a temperature about 13°C (55°F) and when two leaves are showing on the seedlings put them separately into 5 cm (2 in) peat pots. As soon as the roots show through the pots, plant them into the greenhouse border . . . or put out under cloches or into frames. Each transplanting, even in peat pots, will set them back, so make as few moves as possible. This will depend a great deal on the variety, and the weather.

In a greenhouse where the border is used for growing tomatoes during the summer, their place can be taken by lettuce until late March when the new tomato plants are put in. The border must be well dug and dressed with a tomato base fertilizer at 170 g–230 g (6–8 oz) a 0·80 sq m (sq yd), or according to the instructions. Set the seedling plants 17–20 cm (7–8 in) apart, with the lower leaves or rim of the pot slightly above soil level to help avoid botrytis (a disease), by keeping the leaves off the soil. Keep them well watered, about once a week, but less if the weather is damp and dull and try not to water the leaves, as this can cause infection. Early in the day is the best watering time so that the plants are not wet overnight. Lettuce can stand the cold, but it stops their growth and toughens the leaves. The best temperature for winter crops is 7°C–10°C (45–50°F), but if the thermometer shoots above 16°C (60°F) in spring, give them extra ventilation or they will become leggy and heartless.

63

Recommended varieties
For flavour, to raise under glass and plant out of doors:

Balloon	**Little Gem**	**Webb's Wonderful**
Buttercrunch		

Specially bred for growing under glass in winter:

Amanda Plus	**Neptune**	**Vitesse**
Dandie	**Valentine**	**Winter Density**
Kloek		

Mustard and Cress

Too often dismissed as 'kids' stuff' both to eat and to play at growing. The young, in fact, soon tire of the growing game, and it is left to the grown-ups to keep up a constant, and most useful supply. With a little imagination mustard and cress adds life to innumerable hot and cold dishes, far beyond its stick-in-the-mud uses in salads, sandwiches and garnish frills. The botanical name for mustard is *Sinapis alba*, but commercial growers often substitute the quicker growing rape, *Brassica* **64** *napus*. The proper name for cress is *Lepidium sativum*.

Method of growing

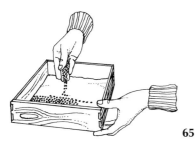

Make sowings every two or three weeks throughout the year. Sow thickly in a seed tray of moist compost, firming the seeds onto it. Or onto a tray of moist sacking or cottonwool (*see drawings 64 and 65*). You should be able to start cutting with scissors within two or three weeks. When mustard and cress are to be used together, sow the cress three days before the mustard. Much will depend on the temperature; 9°C (48°F) will give steady growth. Keep them moist but not soaking. During the summer months the seeds can be grown outside in boxes or small beds **65** of well sifted soil, which must not be allowed to dry out.

Recommended variety
Extra Curled or **Double** Dark green with plenty of curly head and a mild but distinct flavour.

Peas

For temperatures *etc* see table for Beans. Short-growing varieties of peas can be raised and kept in the greenhouse for small early crops. Other varieties can be raised in the greenhouse and set out when all danger of frost is past. Peas can also be set out a little earlier than you would choose for outside plantings, if put under cloches.

Peppers, Sweet (Capsicum)

Sow	Plant	Position	Harvest from	Propa-gation	Temperatures Night min.	Day max.	Notes
early Mar.	mid April	floor of house or pot 17 cm (7 in)	June	24°C (75°F)	16°C (60°F)	21°C (70°F)	Compatible with aubergines and tomatoes

These are expensive to buy and easy to raise from seed. They can be stuffed whole or sliced into salads or any cooked dish. Grow them in pots

66

in a cold greenhouse (*see drawing 66*) or raise them under glass and put them out in sunny, sheltered positions.

Method of growing
Start the seeds off in a temperature of around 24°C (75°F) and transplant into Jiffy pots when they can be handled. They can be grown in pots in a cold greenhouse or under cloches. Plants can also be raised from seed, hardened off and produce well-ripened fruit outdoors in a sunny sheltered position. See also aubergines as the conditions and treatment needed are similar.

Recommended varieties
Ace An early variety, this does well both outdoors and under glass.

Early Prolific Good quality fruit, heavy yield.

Mospa (F1 Hybrid) Produces large blunt-ended, squarish fruits.

Potatoes, Early

No common vegetable can have more gourmet esteem than the first home-grown new potatoes. With a greenhouse this can be as early as Christmas . . . and for the rest of the year they will never taste the same again. There are secrets, mysteries and myths created by the successful growers of these out-of-season treasures, when they produce a few for the family. It is certainly every man to his own potato and method. Here are just a few.

69

67

68

Method of growing

Select 'seed' from your own crop of early potatoes which should have been certified before it was planted. The tubers must be lifted no later than the end of June. Or buy imported new potatoes from the Mediterranean. Choose rather larger 'seed' than you would for a normal outdoor crop. After they have greened a little in the open air, put them in a warm, dry part of the greenhouse to start the shoots sprouting (*see drawing 67*).

Containers Anything which can hold a good depth of soil can be used . . . boxes, large clay or plastic pots, old buckets or cans, so long as there are drainage holes. The sprouted seed should be ready to plant by late August in a light soil. John Innes No 3 compost with an equal quantity of peat is a good mixture. A 25 cm (10 in) pot can accommodate 5 potatoes and a 20 cm (8 in) one, 3 seed tubers. Half fill the containers with compost, put in the seed 5 cm (2 in) deep, and as they grow, cover with more of the same compost until it is within 2–3 cm (1 in) of the top. This allows room for watering. Keep the containers in plenty of light and the compost moist, not wet. As the foliage develops, the water can gradually be increased. (*See drawings 68 and 69.*)

Alternative methods

The sprouted seed can, if convenient, be put into containers in successions to give small crops until the outdoor ones are ready. They can also be sprouted in the greenhouse during winter and then planted under the protection of frames or cloches, remembering the size of the foliage and that in severe frost, they may still by vulnerable. Much will depend on whether you want to spare space in a cold or heated greenhouse.

A simple and easy way for a small family is to put a few sprouted early potatoes into the greenhouse border in February, to eat in early May. The foliage will probably need supporting with strings.

69

Recommended varieties
Use only early ones such as the following, as their haulm is comparatively small and tidy.

Arran Pilot
Epicure
Home Guard
Sharpe's Express

Radishes

Sow	Plant	Position	Harvest from	Propagation	Temperatures		Notes
					Night min.	Day max.	
Jan./Feb. in situ (or where they are to crop)		floor of house	4–6 weeks from planting	(can be grown in unheated houses)	Will fit in with most crops		High temperatures tend to encourage leaf at the expense of roots; good alongside tomatoes

It is oddly contrary of us that we mostly seem to want radishes out of season. As soon as this alluring crisp little root grows in abundance out of doors, we abandon it for new peas, lettuce hearts and the inevitable cucumber and tomato. Perhaps this is partly due to the fact that the radish is so easy to grow that we usually sow far too many seeds at a time, and because there are still some old ones in the ground, forget to sow more before the old ones are completely inedible.

Method of growing
This must be quick, or the roots become 'hot' in flavour and woody in texture. For their true sweet, juicy-nutty taste, they should take no more

70

than six weeks from sowing to pulling, with no set-backs to interrupt their growth. In a cool or slightly heated greenhouse, this can be kept perfectly under control. Sow from January onwards, thinly and in small quantities. They should need no thinning. Use pots, boxes or odd patches of the greenhouse border. Barely cover the seed with soil and never let it get too dry at any stage. As their growing life is so short, they can not afford to be fussy about the soil you give them.

Recommended varieties
Cherry Belle
French Breakfast (*See drawing 70 on previous page.*)
Inca
Long White Icicle Remains sweet and crisp almost indefinitely.

Forced Crops

Yet another advantage of the greenhouse is the opportunity to produce forced delicacies such as chicory and seakale, which are almost always expensive, and fragrant out-of-season mint for your kitchen.

Chicory

Sow	Plant	Position	Harvest from	Propa-gation	Temperatures Night min.	Day max.	Notes
early May to produce roots for forcing	November in succession	under staging in the dark	3–4 weeks after housing dependent on temperature	(Plants grown outdoors from seed)	7°C (45°F) raising to 13°C (55°F)	18°C (68°F)	Can be forced throughout the winter under greenhouse staging

Home grown and blanched chicory, eaten the moment it is cut, has only its appearance to relate it to shop-bought 'chicons'. It is like munching a crisp, nutty apple. Shops, alas, have to show what they are offering and hoping to sell, and daylight ruins both the blanch and flavour of chicory chicons. This is a crop well worth growing as the price scarcely ever seems to drop. Yet it is one of the easiest and most trouble-free vegetables to grow.

Method of growing
There are two easy rules for success; sow at the right time, neither early or late, and blanch them in total darkness . . . not even a chink of light. Sow between early May and early June. You have to use trial and error to get it right for your particular area. Thin the young plants to 22 cm (9 in) apart and then forget about them while they make robust growth resembling perpetual spinach. Don't attempt to eat the bitter leaves, these are to build up the strength of the roots. The chicon you eventually eat is blanched second growth from the mature root.

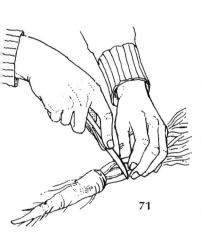

In early October and November cut off the green leaves about 2–3 cm (1 in) above the shoulder of the root (see drawing 71) and lift them carefully. They should be like small parsnips, 5 cm (2 in) thick at the top. Smaller or larger ones do not send up such good heads and are a reproach that you have sown the seed too late or too early. Cut the roots back to 20 cm (8 in), and store in a cool frost-proof place so that they can be used for blanching a few at a time to keep up a supply through the winter.

71

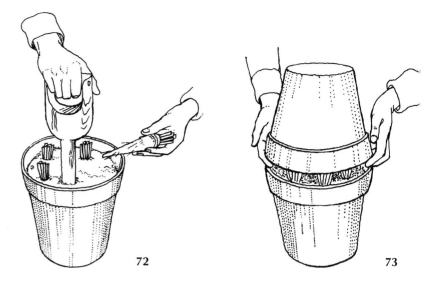

72

73

Forcing

Cut off any sideshoots and pack them upright in deep boxes or pot
about 2–3 cm (1 in) apart (*see drawing 72*). Surround them with moist soi
old compost, peat, sand, or a mixture of all. There are alternative ways o
keeping out the light to blanch the growing chicons.

1 Invert a container of the same size over the pot or box and cover with
sack or black polythene to ensure there are no chinks of light (*see drawin
73*).

2 Cover the crowns with a 17 cm (7 in) layer of dry soil, sand or peat . .
this will keep the chicons hard and compact. Put them under the staging
of the greenhouse and keep in a temperature of 7–13°C (45–55°F). It take
three to four weeks to produce a chicon through the forcing and
blanching process (*see drawing 74*).

Recommended variety

Witloof is the one mostly grown in this country for forcing.

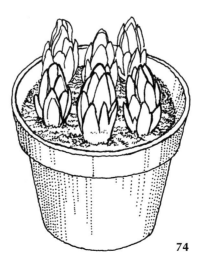

74

Mint

Sow	Plant	Position	Harvest from	Propa-gation	Temperatures Night min.	Day max.	Notes
	Oct. in succession	pots or boxes	3–4 weeks after housing dependent on temperature	Bring in plants grown outdoors	7°C (45°F)	18°C (65°F)	can be grown without heat but results slower

As a well-behaved perennial should, this herb goes into retreat during winter, to recover from the arduous summer. But cooks miss it, and dried mint cannot touch the same taste buds. As they are strenuous growers some of the roots can be sacrificed for winter forcing, so there are fresh shoots through the winter. Lift a few dormant roots at any time from November onwards. Cut them into lengths to fit a seed tray, with 2–3 cm (1 in) of compost below. Cover with about 5 cm (2 in) of fine soil and gently water in. Keep at a temperature of 13°C (55°F). Take up more roots and treat in the same way well before the first batch is used up.

The forced roots will not be worth replanting.

Rhubarb

Sow	Plant	Position	Harvest from	Propa-gation	Temperatures Night min.	Day max.	Notes
	in succession from mid-Nov. on	under staging in the dark	from 3 weeks after housing dependent on temperature	Bring 3 year old crowns from outside	10°C (45°F)	16°C (60°F)	Optimum temperature in the range 10–13°C (50–55°F); rest of the house can be used for crops with similar temperature need

One of the easiest vegetables to force, and one of the most welcome 'fruits' early in the year, very easily persuaded into growth under the staging of a cool greenhouse.

Treatment

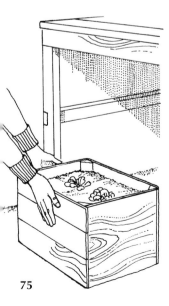

Lift one or more well developed crowns from the garden in November and leave them on the surface to get frosted. This sounds like cruelty, but freezing has a strange relationship with plants, both above and below the surface, including turning starchy root crops into sweeter, more tender ones. In the case of rhubarb it breaks the dormancy of the crown so that in subsequent warmth shoots will grow. Pack the roots close together in deep boxes surrounded by peat or light soil, and exclude all light (*see drawing 75*). The stems will be ready to pull (never cut) in a few weeks.

After any extent of forcing the roots are hardly worth the trouble of returning to the garden to recover. Replacement crowns for forcing are either produced by division of an established plant with each section

75

having a dormant bud on it, or from seed. Crowns should be 3 years old before bringing in for forcing.

Recommended variety
Timperley Early Also a good rhubarb to produce early sticks outdoors especially with a little protection with straw.

Seakale

Sow	Plant	Position	Harvest from	Propa-gation	Temperatures Night min.	Temperatures Day max.	Notes
March	Nov.–Mar. in succession	under staging in the dark	6–3 weeks after the start of forcing as the season progresses	Bring in roots from outside	7°C (45°F) raising to 13°C (55°F)	18°C (68°F)	Roots take 2–3 years to reach forcing size; rest of the house can be used for most crops with similar temperature need

A delectable vegetable which used to be grown widely, but is now regarded as a short-season luxury, like asparagus, but rather more trouble because the shoots have to be blanched, in total darkness. It is not a crop you are likely to find on sale at the local greengrocer's or even in a supermarket, and it is no more arduous to force than rhubarb.

Method of growing
The most economical way is to start from seed . . . if you are prepared to wait two years before you get anything to eat. Seakale needs a permanent bed in well-dug and drained soil enriched with compost or manure, in the sun. For speed, start with 2 year old crowns in March. Plant with the tips just below the surface and give 50 cm (about 18 in) of space around each one. In the Autumn, about November lift the plants, take off the side shoots and branching roots close to the main stem and keep these for re-planting. (See below). Store the main roots (*see drawing 76*) in boxes of damp sand with their crowns exposed in a frost-free (but not warm) place until they are wanted for forcing. Do this in batches as you need them. It takes about 5 or 6 weeks from the time they are brought into the warmth.

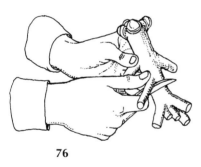

76

77

Forcing
Set the roots upright 7·5 cm (3 in) apart in pots or boxes at least 22 cm (9 in) deep. Pack them with old compost or a mixture of garden soil and peat, leave the crowns just exposed (*see drawing 77*), water them, shut out all light leaving space for the crowns to grow stems 15–22 cm (6–9 in) tall – black polythene bags are useful for this purpose – and put the container under the greenhouse staging. A temperature of 7–13°C (45–55°F) suits them best; it should not exceed 18°C (68°F) in any case

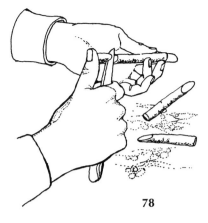

78

Root cuttings

After being forced the seakale crowns are exhausted and fit only for the compost heap, but new plants can be grown from the trimmed side roots. After removing them from the parent plant, choose straight pencil-thick roots, 7–12 cm (3–5 in) long (*see drawing 78*). Cut them straight across the top and make a slanting cut at the bottom, so you can tell which way up to plant them. Tie in bundles and store upright in damp sand in a frost-free shed or garage. By March their tops will have formed buds and they can be planted outside until it is their turn in November for the forcing treatment.

Note Not all the crowns need be forced in warmth. Some can be left outside and covered with large pots or boxes in succession. Be sure to exclude all light or the shoots will be bitter. Cut these individually as they grow.

Part 2

Running Your Greenhouse

Previously we have been dealing mainly with the raising of individual crops. Here we are concerned with one of the most useful functions of the greenhouse – raising seed under its shelter until the seedlings are ready to put outside. The use of cloches and cold frames follows, and after this comes advice on the general care involved in running your greenhouse; how to avoid trouble – and how to cope with it if it occurs – and lastly, a month-by-month reminder of 'what happens, when'.

Raising Seed for Outdoors

Raising plants from seed in the greenhouse is both easy and economical. Most of the everyday vegetables which need an early start will tolerate a wide range of temperatures and will not need artificial heat. They can be brought into sturdy setting-out seedling stage, just with sun and protection. This will vary from one part of the country to another. Seeds in a greenhouse come up with such alacrity, that you have to guard against becoming slapdash. Seedlings may appear rapidly in profusion, but to sustain them for their expected life span, there must be some 'before care' and 'after care'. Prepare everything in advance, making a start by cleaning pots, boxes and trays which have been used before.

Plants which resent being transplanted, like sweetcorn and ridge cucumbers, are best sown in small peat blocks. These, when they germinate, are transplanted whole in their little nests, into larger peat pots and then into their eventual growing places.

Preparing the compost

Before you start, it is vital to ensure that peat-based seed composts are in the right moist, but not soggy, condition before seeds can be sown. If the bags of compost have been opened and become dry they must be soaked overnight, preferably in clean rain water. Overdry peat will float and must be left for hours in a bucket with a little water in the bottom to soak up until it becomes crumbly and the texture of moist bread crumbs. If, next day, you can still wring water out of a handful, you must leave the compost until the excess moisture has evaporated because too wet is as damaging as too dry.

Sowing

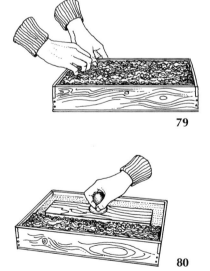

Fill the box almost to the rim, pressing well into the ends and corners of boxes, level and gently firm the compost (see drawings 79 and 80). Sow the seed very thinly either broadcast or in rows so that the seedlings have room to develop. Overcrowding makes them 'leggy' and they will not develop into useful plants unless 'pricked out' very quickly (see below). Press the seeds gently into the surface, and unless they are very tiny, sprinkle over them a fine covering of the same compost, and lightly spray the surface to settle it. You can leave the seeds to germinate in their own time in the greenhouse out of the sun, or use a propagator to hurry them up. Cover the seedtray with a sheet of glass, then brown paper to keep out the light. Take a daily peep and the moment the seed growth breaks surface, remove the paper, raise the glass so that air can circulate and remove it completely in a day or two. (See drawing 11 on page 22.)

For the seed sown early in the year in a greenhouse, a temperature during the day of around 16°C (60°F) should keep the seedlings growing steadily. Water sparingly but never let the compost dry out.

Pricking out

What you do with your newly germinated seedlings must depend entirely on their breed and your plans for their future.

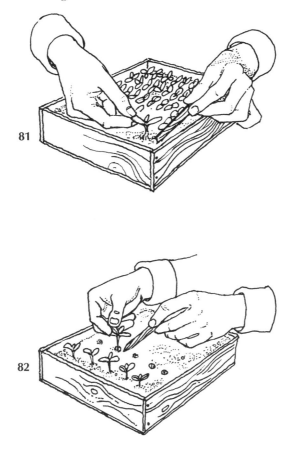

81

82

83

Transplant the seedlings as soon as they are large enough to be held by a single leaf, *not* the stem (*see drawing 81*) before they have used up the nourishment in their sowing compost, or they will become woody and the foliage yellow. What they need as soon as possible is the mature diet of a potting compost. Fill the pots or boxes in advance, hold a leaf of the seedling in the fingers of one hand, and with the other, carefully loosen the roots with a smooth piece of cane, wood, spoon handle, or anything suitable (*see drawing 82*). In one movement, lift and transfer the plant into its more nourishing growing home and make the roots firm by pressing with the fingers. Water them in and keep in a humid, but not stuffy, atmosphere for a few days (*see drawing 83*). Keep in a well-lit part of the house and if they are to be grown outside, gradually move them to cooler parts of the greenhouse so that they can gradually get used to less pampered living. You must use your own judgement in deciding when plants are finally 'hardened off'. There are no rules. Indoor and outdoor conditions can vary tremendously.

Plants which are going to remain indoors need no hardening-off, but still must be kept close to the glass in their early life so that they do not become drawn and lanky. Those seeds which were planted into little blocks because they hate any root disturbance can be grown on in soil blocks of John Innes potting compost.

CROPPING CHART

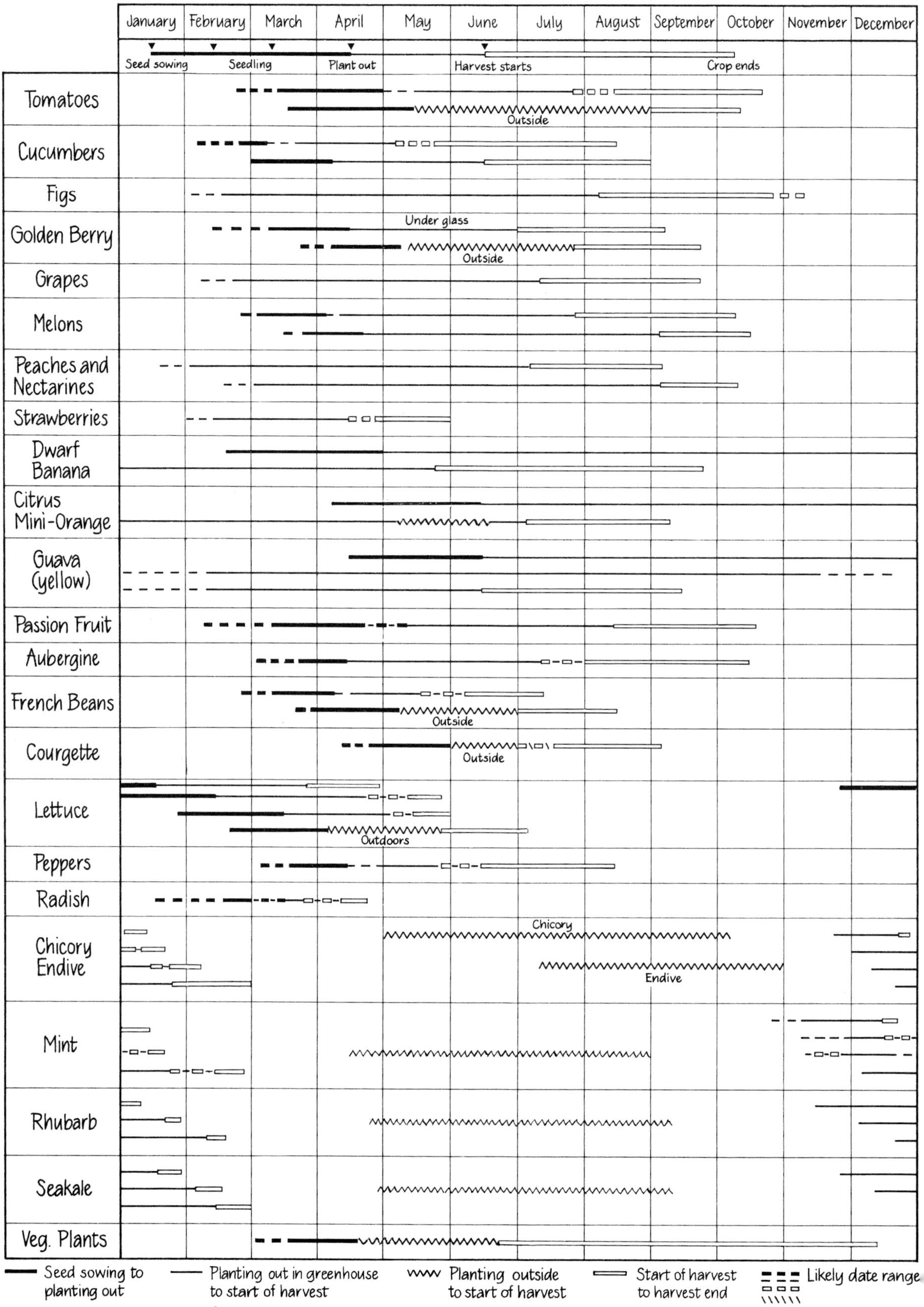

	January	February	March	April	May	June	July	August	September	October	November	December

Seed sowing   Seedling   Plant out   Harvest starts   Crop ends

Tomatoes
Outside

Cucumbers

Figs

Golden Berry
Under glass
Outside

Grapes

Melons

Peaches and Nectarines

Strawberries

Dwarf Banana

Citrus Mini-Orange

Guava (yellow)

Passion Fruit

Aubergine

French Beans
Outside

Courgette
Outside

Lettuce
Outdoors

Peppers

Radish

Chicory Endive
Chicory
Endive

Mint

Rhubarb

Seakale

Veg. Plants

―― Seed sowing to planting out   ― Planting out in greenhouse to start of harvest   ∿∿ Planting outside to start of harvest   ▭ Start of harvest to harvest end   ▬ ▬ ▬ Likely date range

82

Plants which are to be put outdoors for part of their lives, especially in spring when outdoor conditions can be quite inhospitable, need more attention to hardening off. This will take longer if the plants have been raised with heat because they need to be gradually accustomed first to unheated conditions inside, then to outside temperatures. An unheated frame can be very useful for this (see *Cloches and Cold Frames*). The glass can be taken off by day and only replaced if frost threatens at night. For plants which basically are hardy a few days of these conditions should ensure that the plants have hardened off, *ie* that they will endure a slight frost without any damage, and at that stage they can be put out in their final quarters without risk.

Brassicas

This family includes such popular vegetables as cabbage, cauliflower, Brussels sprouts, kale and broccoli. Most of them need a long growing season, which means an early start in the greenhouse, so they can gather strength through the summer, and some can survive the winter and following spring and at the same time produce most welcome crops. Only those members of the family which will benefit from an early coddled upbringing, will be mentioned here. Others will give their best if grown from start to finish out of doors.

Brussels Sprouts

Extremely hardy, these crop continuously from as early as August to March. Even when smothered for weeks under a deep blanket of snow, they will be in perfect condition if you can locate them. Far better than being exposed to the hungry winter eye of pigeons and other birds. But to reach and maintain the stamina for such a performance, they must have a long body-building season. The sooner you can start them off, the sturdier they will be.

Sowing and planting Start sowing them in the greenhouse from the end of January if this suits your plans, but March will still give you plenty of time. It will depend on the variety you choose . . . early or late; how soon the outdoor ground will be ready for the plants, and how long you can spare it to them. Sow in 10 cm (4 in) deep boxes on trays and thin out the seedlings to 4 cm (1½ in) apart. Harden off so they can be planted out in early April 60 cm (2 ft) apart into rich, firm soil. Tread around the stems after planting. If allowed to rock around in loose soil and a high wind they will produce large, open sprouts, and rain may collect around the neck, become frozen, and rot the stem.

Cabbage

By planting different varieties to mature at various times, you can be cutting cabbages all through the year. There are varieties for spring and early summer; for autumn and for winter. A good, illustrated seed catalogue will help you choose. Many can be sown into outdoor seedbeds, but to get the tight, crispy, tangy head of modern summer cabbage in May, you need to start them in a greenhouse.

Sowing and planting From late January onwards sow in 10 cm (4 in) deep boxes or trays of seed compost. When the seedlings are big enough to handle thin them to about 4 cm (1½ in) apart. Harden off and plant out when they are 7·5 cm (3 in) tall. Space them about 40 cm (15 in) apart. This can vary, particularly with new varieties, so take the seedman's advice.

Cauliflower

This name now applies also to winter varieties which were formerly called broccoli, while broccoli is now used for the very hardy, looser-growing kinds which are known as 'sprouting broccoli.' Cauliflowers are more tender with a most delicate flavour.

Cauliflowers are one of the small group of vegetables which become distressed by root disturbance and sulk, almost to death, when they are transplanted. You cannot just pick them up by a leaf and drop the roots into a hole in the open ground, then firm them in. They must be grown so that when they are ready to be planted outside, their roots are encased in a block of compost.

Sowing Start sowing the greenhouse seeds in January for the summer varieties, using boxes or trays as for the other brassicas already described. But thin them out more harshly so that they are at least 5 cm (2 in) apart each way. This will keep their roots from intermingling, so that they can be transplanted in small individual blocks.

Growing Keep them well watered, harden off, and transplant in April when the little plants have about six leaves and are roughly 7·5 cm (3 in) tall. To ease the transplanting trauma, cut the seedbox compost into blocks with a sharp knife, resembling a crossword puzzle, each block holding the roots of one seedling. Choose a day when the soil is moist, and set them 60 cm (2 ft) apart each way into rich, well-dug soil. Put the seedlings in at the depth they were in the seed tray, not buried, and water them in. Take care that they are never short of water, especially in the early stages, or small heads will quickly form which is a sign that the plant has gone to seed. To protect the curds (heads) from strong sunlight, bend a few outer leaves over them as they develop.

Celery

The two types of celery are *trench*, either white, pink or red; and *self-blanching*, green, yellow or golden. The first must be grown in trenches in a rich deep soil, is not easy to grow, and takes time and trouble (see Growing, opposite). It is up to you whether the result is worth the effort. The white types have the best flavour but are the least hardy. For a late crop, choose the hardier pink or red celery.

Self-blanching varieties take the hard work out of growing this crop. They do not need trenching and take up little space as they are planted in blocks, not rows, 22 cm (9 in) apart each way, so that the stems are blanched by the plants being grown closely together (*see drawing 84*). Their disadvantage is that they are less tasty (though thankfully also less stringy) and must be dug up before frosts start. The first sticks should be ready in

84

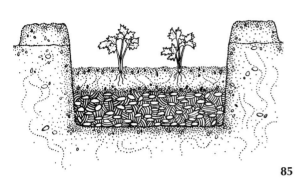

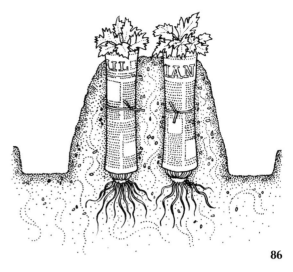

85

86

September and used at once. Never let them go short of moisture or the stems will grow tough and stringy.

Sowing The seed is small and germinates slowly. Sow the seeds at the end of February for an early crop, and March for a later one. The seed must be sown early enough to make good sized, hardened-off plants to be set outside in late May or early June. Sow thinly in seed boxes and as soon as they are big enough to handle, transplant the seedlings into deeper boxes of potting compost, in which they can remain to be hardened-off and then planted out. Don't leave the seedlings too long in their seed tray and compost, or they will become 'hard' and may run to seed outside in a dry summer. Alternatively transplant into peat blocks for less root disturbance at transplanting.

Trench celery Celery is a hungry, thirsty crop. Give a liquid feed during the summer and plenty of water in dry weather. Trench varieties are planted in a trench about 15 cm (6 in) deep, with plenty of bulky compost or old manure under it. Space the plants about 30 cm (1 ft) apart and blanch them when 30 cm (1 ft) high by removing any side shoots, wrap the stems with newspapers or collars, and partly fill the trench with soil originally taken from it. At the end of August mound moist soil against the stems and in mid-September complete earthing up to form a mound with only the tops of the foliage showing (*see drawings 85 and 86*). It is best not to lift the blanched varieties until there has been a sharp frost, as this makes the plant crisper and sweeter. This should usually be possible by early November, depending on your local climate.

Onions

The large, exhibition-size bulbs which will not rot while stored in winter insist on a long growing season. In some parts of the country 'sets' rather than seeds are popular, but they are only available in a limited range of varieties and the growing season is not long enough to give the largest sizes. Raising the seed under glass before the outside conditions are friendly is the only way to ensure a long season of growth.

Sowing Don't buy too much seed if you have little outdoor space. 25 g (1 oz) seed produces enough plants for a 30 m (33 yd) row spaced at 15 cm (6 in) apart. You could most likely sell or barter the overflow to friends. Sow from mid-January in deep boxes of seed compost. Don't waste seed by being heavy-handed as the seedlings have to be thinned out eventually to 2–3 cm (1 in) apart. Sprinkle only a light covering of compost over the seed. Harden off in late March for planting out.

Planting out Take out only a few seedlings at a time from the box so the roots are not exposed to a drying wind or sun. The roots must fall neatly and vertically into the planting hole, with the base of the bulb about 1 cm (½ in) below the surface, so that the other bulbous half is above the ground. Plant firmly.

When the crop is nearing maturity, the foliage will keel over; leave for a few weeks. Then fork under each one to break the roots. A week or so later lift on a dry day and leave on soil to complete drying, before storing in an airy shed.

Leeks

These need a long growing season and are at their best started early under glass. There are early, mid-season and late varieties, and only the early ones need the greenhouse care, so that they will reach their maximum size by August . . . which is important if you want to exhibit at the local show, or make Vichyssoise, that renowned cold summer soup. Sow the seed in February in 10 cm (4 in) deep boxes, harden off and plant outside during April.

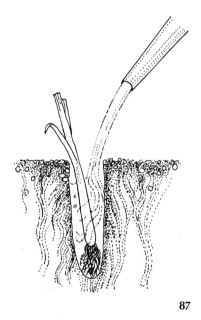

87

Planting Leeks are not as demanding as onions about soil fertility. They will grow almost anywhere which is not actually under water. They are best in ground which has been manured for a previous crop. Make a hole with a dibber or trowel about 15 cm (6 in) deep, drop in the baby leek and, dribble by dribble, gently fill the hole with water to settle the roots (see drawing 87). *Never* fill the hole with soil. Plant 15–22 cm (6–9 in) apart in rows 30 cm (1 ft) apart.

Maintenance Leeks are always lapping up water. Give them plenty during dry spells so they can put on flesh, otherwise they will remain small, and stay tough and woody after cooking. To get an extra length of white 'blanched' stem, gently draw up dry, not wet, soil around them when they have got into their growing stride and are no longer seedlings.

Sweetcorn

Outdoor sowings are not reliable except in the more sheltered, hot, sunny and windless areas . . . hard to find outside the south and south-east of England. So many remain immature at the end of summer, fit only for compost. Sweetcorn is notorious for going into a sulky decline after any root disturbance. The best solution is to sow the seeds individually into 7·5 cm (3 in) peat pots, ranged on a tray in the greenhouse, or for safety, two seeds per pot, removing the weakest if they both germinate. Sow mid-April to early May, keeping the peat seed pots always moist.

Growing Plant out when there is no chance of further frost . . . always in a block, not straight rows, however small, so that they pollinate closely. In a straight row, and even a half-hearted wind, the pollen from the masthead (the only male flower) can be literally cast to the winds. Cover surface roots which appear with soil or compost. Harvest when the top 'silk' turns from golden to brown. With experience one can judge when this coincides with all but the topmost kernels being mature. This can only be seen by peeling back the wrapper leaves which often lets birds in to attack the cobs, so they are best judged by look and feel of the cob and the appearance of the silks.

Chitting (or sprouting) Potatoes
In February set out the seed potatoes in shallow boxes or egg trays with the 'rose' end uppermost. (This is the wide and broader end which produces the nest egg, as it were, of growing 'eyes'). Keep in full light away from the sun, and plant out when the shoots are a sturdy 1–3 cm (about ½–1 in) long, usually early in March. Where there are more than two sprouting shoots, keep the two strongest. These will not be damaged when put into open soil, and will provide the best crop. (*See also page 70.*)

Tomatoes
See Tomatoes, page 22, for method of raising seeds.

Planting Plants should be hardened off before being put outside and then put out only after the risk of frost is over, spaced about 45 cm (18 in) apart according to variety. The bush types which require no staking, stopping or side shooting need about 15 cm (6 in) more space each way than do the other varieties which are grown very much like those under glass. Careful choice of a sheltered spot will have a big effect on results, the amount of protection deciding both size of crop and its earliness. Having raised the plants under glass they can be out under glass or polythene cloches and this will give a good start. If the whole life of the crop can be spent under protection, so much the better.

Growing Positioning against a south-facing wall will give satisfactory results in most seasons, with four or five trusses of fruit being ripened. Varieties which need to have their side shoots removed should be supported with canes or string. If covered throughout their life with cloches, the plants will need to be trained horizontally. The fruit will then be subject to soil splashing so a covering of straw over the soil is advisable, to prevent this. Plants which are being trained up stakes outdoors may as well be stopped in mid-August so that the fruit will have a chance to ripen before the frost. At the end of the season, unfasten plants from their supports, lay them on a bed of straw and cover with cloches to ripen the fruit. The very last of the crop can be brought indoors while still green to ripen on a warm windowsill.

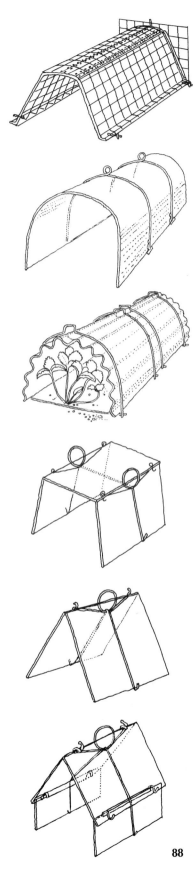

Cloches and Cold Frames

The name of this useful type of gardening equipment originates from the bell-shaped glass covers used for forcing and protecting outdoor plants in the 18th and 19th century. (It was also borrowed to describe one of the least flattering hat shapes for women.) In its garden context it is in essence a portable plant protection which extends the outdoor season at both ends. Cloches can be used as half-way rest homes between greenhouse and open garden; for warming up soil before seeds or seedlings are sown or planted, and in dozens of ingenious ways. Here are a few of them.

Making use of cloches

Cloches are useful for giving an early start to salads and tender vegetables, raised from seed in the greenhouse, when their space is needed before they are strong enough to withstand unfriendly weather. Once they have settled and there is no frost danger, the cloches can be whipped off for another job of protection; lettuce or sweetcorn are examples. They can also be used for greenhouse-raised plants which are too boisterous for a small house, but also too timid to do well in an open garden, such as melon; or again, for greenhouse-raised plants which do very well in the open when the nights as well as days are warm, but which have to be banished from home early because space is needed for a growing generation such as early runner beans. Cloches can also be used to cover up outdoor strawberries so they fruit well ahead of normal time. Put them over the young plants at the end of February. Polythene tunnels are well suited for this purpose although glass cloches give slightly earlier (7–10 days) fruit ripening. Lastly, to help outdoor tomatoes to ripen in late July and early August, remove their supports, lay them on straw and cover with cloches. Flowers which set after this time may well not ripen so the plants should be stripped by removing a proportion of the lower leaves to speed ripening before the cloches are put over the plants.

Types of cloche

These have multiplied and diversified out of all recognition from the original 'bell jars'. They are now in all weatherproof materials; all shapes, heights, lengths, self-watering types, and prices. The choice is yours; some of the alternatives are shown here (*drawings 88 and 89*).

Plastic, rigid or flexible plastic and polythene has almost completely replaced the more difficult to handle and expensive glass. Rigid plastic lasts longer, but the flexible tunnel type of polythene sheet, stretched over a wire frame is simpler to roll back when the plants need treatment, and easier to roll up and store when not in use. They are not suitable though for individual protection. Individual plant protectors comprising a circular frame covered with a polythene bag can be put over a melon, or capsicum or a rare squash, when there is suddenly a hint of frost in the air, in either early spring or a too-soon autumn.

88

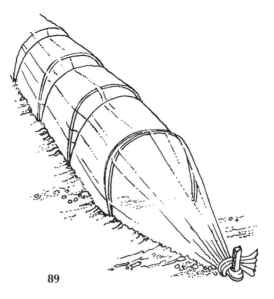

89

Making use of a cold frame

A most useful adjunct to the greenhouse where plants can be hardened off by slowly letting more air into the frame each day, raising the lights gradually until they can be removed completely, and the seedlings or plants set out in the garden. Apart from being a stepping-stone from the greenhouse to the open garden, a frame can be used to raise continuous salad crops; shelter crops in winter; grow tender crops which have been raised in the greenhouse, such as golden berry, melon, cucumber, tomatoes, sweet pepper (capsicum), and aubergine (egg plant). According to your taste, and space. When that so-often-delayed moment comes, when it is vital to have a greenhouse clean-out, pots, boxes and any movable containers full of plants can be stored in a frame while the work is done.

Types of cold frame

A frame is simply a box outdoors, covered with a glass lid which can be opened as you please. In its traditional form the 'box' was made of wood **90a** concrete or brick. The handy man can make his own from junk yard

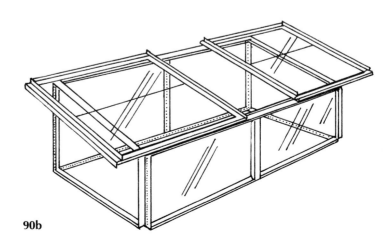

90b

91

plunder, using discarded window for the 'lights.' Modern ones can b
bought in all sizes and materials. The standard design of frame slopes s
that taller plants can be protected at the back, with the smallest at th
front . . . like a school photograph. They can be bought made entirely c
glass with an aluminium frame; of corrugated plastic sheets with a ligh
wooden framework; or of tough plastic sheeting. These have th
advantage of being portable, but give much less protection and are easil
damaged – they can be bowled over in a high wind or destroyed by
falling branch. The only damage likely to be caused to a solic
permanent frame, is the odd broken pane which is easily replaced. The
can also be heated with special air- or soil-warming electric cables and thi
increases their value considerably (*see drawings 90a, 90b and 91*).

Routine Care in the Greenhouse

Making a success of your greenhouse, will depend, to a large extent, on the care with which routine jobs are done. For busy people who are away during the middle of the day on, perhaps, five days in the week, some thought should be given to means of 'automating' heating (if required), ventilation and watering; see pages 120–125 for details of equipment. All these are important and if they are neglected, perhaps by leaving the ventilators closed when the day turns out to be a warm one and temperatures go too high – crops will suffer; indeed, they can die from the combined effects of high temperatures and lack of water and, of course, the overall results will be disappointing.

Heating without waste

The cost of heating has to be balanced against the pleasure in growing particular crops and their value compared with what can be bought, even though of inferior quality. Electricity is probably the easiest to control but expensive. At the other extreme is paraffin and here there have been developments in recent years in the direction of better control of temperature. The temperatures which can be maintained in the house, of course, depend on the plants being grown. The tables which are given with each crop show minimum values for good results. With mixed cropping, a compromise has to be worked out and, in general, most plants grown in a community with others with a slightly different temperature requirement will be happier with a slightly higher temperature than the one recommended. In practice, most houses are heated for the period October till April when, given attention to making best use of the greenhouse space, the greatest benefits will be obtained. On grounds of economy, the temperatures aimed for in this period may be less than optimum for some crops and in these circumstances it is better to delay growing them until weather conditions improve because a number, such as tomatoes and cucumbers, will not grow as well as they should at temperatures much below the ones indicated. For some owners, the temperatures aimed for are 10–13°C (50–55°F) by day and 4–17°C (40–45°F) by night which are too low for many plants to thrive. These are, however, reasonable temperatures for vegetable plants in particular to be raised for subsequent planting outside, especially if a propagator is available to give higher temperatures for germination. These propagators enable higher temperatures to be maintained in a restricted volume and so they are more economical than attempting to heat the whole house. Also, as a result of being inside the greenhouse, they do not require as much heat to maintain the desired temperatures as if they are outside. More information on the use of propagators is given on page 124.

A more economical alternative than maintenance of high temperatures is to keep the house frost-free over winter in order to allow plants like geraniums to survive. Then to start heating in the spring when, as the sun gains strength, and temperatures start to rise, the temperature 'lift' in the greenhouse is not as great; lift is the difference between outside and inside temperatures.

As temperatures rise by day with the sun the heating should be switched off as a first step to stopping temperatures going too high and to economize on fuel. Not only is this wasteful in heat if temperatures go too high in the spring, but, of course, plants can be damaged if the temperatures go much above the recommended maximums.

Ventilation

With lengthening days, ventilation may have to be started to control temperatures. This is easy to do if there is someone on hand able to keep an eye on the greenhouse and to adjust the ventilators as temperatures change. Those on the leeward side should be opened first, any lower ones before those in the roof. If this is not sufficient to maintain temperatures at the required level, then more ventilators should be opened, progressing to the lower ventilators on the windward side. Finally, open the upper ventilators on the windward side. Ventilators usually have some adjustment on them and the ventilators should be opened progressively to keep temperatures within the required limits.

If the house has to be left in the morning then ventilators have to be opened early in anticipation of the weather of the day and the tell-tale of the maximum thermometer gives some idea of what temperatures have been like during the day. Of course, this does not indicate whether the maximum was held for most of the day or only reached for a few minutes but, at least, it gives some indication of what the plants have had to put up with and can be linked with the amount of water that they have used during the day as a guide to how much water is needed at the next watering.

The aim in ventilation is to have air movement without draughts causing leaves to move violently. Ventilation ought to be done especially carefully early in the season when plants are tender. Regular ventilation by day is probably going to be needed from March onwards through to October and by May, some ventilation even by night is a good idea.

Automatic ventilators

As with other forms of automatic control, the automatic ventilator is a great help in dealing with unexpected changes in the weather. If this equipment is fitted on the lee side of the house, then there is less likely to be any draught on plants but of recent years the prevailing winds in spring have often tended to come from the east rather than the west so it is difficult to choose which is the leeward side of the house. The type of automatic ventilator which depends on a cylinder reacting to the temperatures around it is certainly helpful although not ideal because, particularly in the spring, most crops are growing in the floor of the house and so some distance from the cylinder. The roof of the house is always the warmest because warm air rises and houses equipped with this type of automatic ventilator will be ventilated according to the temperature in the roof rather than the temperature at the crop. Nevertheless, they are a big improvement on not having any automatic aids at all because they will open if temperatures get high. They will also close again, of course, as temperatures fall in the evening. With ventilators opened by hand, it is a good idea, especially in spring, to close houses down early so that some sun heat is trapped in the house.

In these days of greater awareness of heat conservation, greenhouses cannot be regarded as very efficient. It is well worth while before starting the season to check round all the gaps in construction to make sure these are sealed so that what heat is in the house is kept there for as long as possible especially in the evening as outside temperatures start to fall. Double glazing is worth considering although there are certain drawbacks; see page 120 for further discussion.

Where electricity is available in the greenhouse, another form of ventilation is by fan. This is controlled by a thermostat so that it only operates when required. This type of ventilation is useful in spring to deal with the occasional burst of sunshine but wasteful of energy in summer and if the electric fan is the only form of ventilation, it is probably unable to keep the house cool enough in high summer when, on occasions, doors as well as windows may have to be fully opened in order to keep temperatures down to reasonable levels. Many small greenhouses tend to be undersupplied with movable ventilators and where additional ventilators can be bought as an extra, they are often very well worthwhile.

Problems of the small greenhouse

The relatively small volumes of air in small greenhouses heat up rapidly but also cool down rapidly. In terms of ventilation, summer temperatures under glass can be too high for many crops and with shade temperatures in the 'eighties', greenhouse temperatures can be, perhaps, 20°F higher than this with consequent increases in plant temperatures and water requirement. This is why the spring is the peak time for greenhouse use in the gap between the damaging frosts of winter outside and the scorching heat of summer. Shading the glass can be a help as well as damping down the floor of the house, especially in the morning. This cools the atmosphere by evaporation of moisture. The smaller the house the more excessive temperature ranges tend to be. Polythene houses heat quickly because of their more airtight construction compared with the overlapping panes of glass in the conventional greenhouse. Polythene houses also cool quickly because they do not retain heat at night which is released from the soil after it has been heated by the sun's rays during the day. For this reason an unheated polythene house cannot be used for cropping as early in the year as an unheated glass house because of the loss of heat.

Unheated houses probably need more careful ventilation than heated ones, otherwise, the range from overnight minimum to mid-afternoon maximum is too great. To some extent and for some crops like tomato, high day temperatures can compensate for low night temperatures but these should not be outside the ranges specified in the tables.

Watering

This has been referred to several times already and is an important routine job. Plants in the greenhouse will require much more water when in active growth than when dormant and watering cannot be neglected in the summer otherwise plants can die in a short space of time. For this reason, automatic watering devices (see page 124) ought to be considered as a means both of reducing the time which has to be spent on this job and ensuring that plants are watered when they need it, not when you can manage it.

To some extent, the need for water can be affected by the way in which crops are grown. If they are in the soil in the base of the house, then the roots will be able to explore a larger volume of soil in search of moisture and have a reserve to draw on in case the next application of water is delayed. It is worthwhile helping plants to form extensive root systems by planting into uniformly moist soil at the start of the season and then holding back on water in the early stages of growth so that the roots grow out in search for it. If water is applied heavily from the time of planting, then there is no need for the plants to grow a large root system and in consequence they will need more frequent watering at times of peak demand. They are also more vulnerable to extremes of temperature because there is not the reserve in the soil which they can draw on. The summer demand for moisture by a crop like tomato should not be underestimated. The table gives an indication of the requirement per plant in the mid-summer period for the average temperatures which these conditions imply.

Recommended watering quantities for (say) tomatoes

Daytime Weather Conditions	Water Requirement/Plant/Day
Dull, overcast, cloudy	150 ml–300 ml (¼–½ pt)
Dull and overcast for most of the day, occasional bright periods	300 ml–450 ml (½–¾ pt)
Dull periods interspersed with bright sunshine	568 ml–750 ml (1–1¼ pt)
Sunny for most of the day	750 ml–1·1 l (1¼–2 pt)
Bright and sunny all day	1·1 l–1·4 l (2–2½ pt)

From the table it will be apparent that a tomato plant will require amounts up to 9 l (2 gall) of water per plant per week from April to September; a considerable volume of water which normally has to come from the mains. Liquid feeds can be added according to the crop and are a very convenient way of applying fertilizer. Many of the proprietary liquid fertilizers are suitable for a range of greenhouse plants and the manufacturers' recommendations should be followed regarding rate of use, frequency of application, *etc.*

Plants may not be in the border soil but in a pot or on a raised bed or on staging. In this case, they are much more dependent on small, but regular watering. Roots may be less easily damaged by overwatering when growing in a proprietary compost because it is designed with drainage in mind but are more liable to dry out in warm weather. This also applies to plants in peat growing bags or pots on the surface of the soil or ring culture and greater amounts of water than those in the table may well be needed. More to the point, more frequent applications may need to be made because of the limited capacity of the pot or container to hold water. It is always advisable to leave, perhaps, a watering space of about 1 cm (½ in) at the top of each pot in which water can be put to drain through as the compost in the container absorbs the water. Even this, however, is not sufficient to carry plants which do not have extensive root systems, through a very bright day. Automation of watering systems applies to plants on staging using, perhaps, capillary matting. But for reasons of high temperature and increased water demand, many crops which can be grown under glass in summer can more easily be managed outside where temperatures are less extreme and rainfall helps to meet water needs. Here again, then, is further justification for making the spring the main period of use of the greenhouse.

While on the subject of water, too much is more harmful to most plants than too little. The plant which is wilting due to shortage of water is easily cured and usually responds overnight. Overwatering, on the other hand, can aggravate soil-borne diseases and the superficial conclusion that the plant needs more water because it is wilting often makes the situation worse. Plants with damaged roots are much more difficult to help. They do not have the roots to absorb either moisture or nutrients and do not always respond well to occasional drying out of the soil. In the case of tomato, plants produce fresh roots at the soil surface and, given proper treatment like covering with fresh, moistened compost this will encourage these roots to grow out and eventually take over support of the plant. The plant growing in border soil (where glass to the ground is necessary so that light reaches plants at soil level), is cushioned against either under- or over-watering, especially if it is well drained. The early management that is aimed at developing strong root systems on plants is a further means of avoiding later problems with water.

How to tell when plants need water
The appearance of plants is usually the best indicator, but, for someone who is not used to them, this fact is not always very helpful. The healthy plant is upright, dark green, growing well (dependent on temperature). The plant which is dry (but the same is also true of the plant with a damaged root system) tends to be dull in colour with flagging leaves, especially at midday and growth is poor or non-existent.

The appearance of the soil surface can also give some indication. It looks dry and light in colour when there is probably need for water or wet and dark in colour when water has been applied recently. Sometimes the situation can be reached where crops are growing in the floor of the house and the plants themselves are indicating they are dry but yet the surface of the soil appears wet. This occurs particularly where hoses are used for watering and over a period of weeks, or perhaps months, fine particles get washed in between the coarser ones so that the surface soil becomes quite sealed. Then the water which is applied appears to lie about for a long time and the conclusion that may be drawn, quite wrongly, is that the soil is full of water. Indeed, sometimes it can be very dry under the sealed surface layer and the only way to find out is to dig down carefully mid-way between plants to see if the soil is wet or dry.

How to check for dry soil

The test of whether the soil is holding sufficient moisture or not is to hold a small amount in the palm of the hand. Close the hand up and then release it again. The soil is in the correct condition if it just stays moulded in the shape left by the palm and fingers. If too dry, it will not retain its shape but will fall apart as soon as the pressure on it is released. If too wet, then it may even be possible to wring water out of the soil. Certainly, it will retain its shape once the fingers are released and will look too wet. When the soil is behaving in the right way, then it is said to be in 'potting' condition.

Where crops are growing in pots, then again the appearance of the plants and of the surface of the soil are good indicators of dryness. The weight of the pot is another indication and its 'ring' when struck with the knuckles or a piece of wood. The soil which is wet returns a thud, whereas when the plant needs watering, the pot has a ring to it. This can only be learnt by experience. Another way of gauging the need for water is from the table included on page 94 for, for instance, tomato, digging in to the soil at, perhaps, 10-day intervals with a trowel to check whether adequate quantities are getting down to the roots. With a crop like cucumbers, watering of the roots is less important than maintaining a humid atmosphere around the above-ground parts of plants. Cucumber beds are normally raised up on the floor of the house to provide very quick drainage and it is more difficult to judge when watering is needed. The heavy applications of water which are needed in the house to maintain the correct growing atmosphere will go a long way, however, to meet the water needs of the plant and, although possibly, daily watering of the beds is required, the appearance of the plants and their rate of growth has to be the ultimate test. Instruments are available to indicate the state of the moisture supply in the soil and can be useful when the gardener gets used to 'reading' the plants. When using automatic watering devices (see page 124) it becomes that much easier to overwater, particularly if the system is only semi-automatic and relies on someone turning the tap off! An advantage of some of the drip methods of watering, however, is that the surface panning which has already been described is much less likely to occur. The water will radiate in a cone underneath each nozzle and as long as the position of these is not changed during the growing season then plants usually develop a root system which enables them to make use of the water which is being applied by this method.

The healthy greenhouse

The basis of hygiene in the greenhouse is the use of sterilized composts for raising young plants. These are freed of pests and diseases which can attack plants once they have germinated and are at their most vulnerable. The soil in the floor of the house can harbour pests and diseases and with repeated growing of the same crop year by year the soil becomes 'sick' as a result. The symptoms of this are that growth declines and yields are poor; remedial measures have to be taken and these are either not readily available to amateur greenhouse owners or are expensive. Re-soiling houses is of doubtful value. Only shallow removal of soil gives merely limited improvement – say one or two years better cropping. Partial sterilization with formaldehyde is reasonably effective but the house has to be empty for a period of weeks because of the fumes. Growing crops in peat bags or pots on the soil surface or by ring culture is effective but limits the height of the house available for cropping, is more expensive and more troublesome over watering. So it is worthwhile trying to delay the time when these measures become necessary for as long as possible.

Acquiring good habits

Here are some steps you can take to keep your greenhouse healthy.

1 *Practise rotation round the house* so that the same crop is grown in different parts over a three or four year cycle.

2 *Try to keep plants healthy* by looking after them properly; remove any which die mysteriously. Take them out of the house including the root system and the soil around it, taking care not to spill any in the rest of the house.

3 *Dispose of suspect plants as far away as possible from the greenhouse* so that they will be unlikely to contaminate the rest of the house. Pick up dead leaves and destroy them. At the end of the season take out as much of the old plant as possible including its root system.

4 *Burn rather than compost* such residues to avoid the risk that any problems might come back in to the greenhouse.

5 *Watch for pests and diseases* and control them as they happen. Not only will this be of direct benefit to the crop at the time, but if these problems are neglected spores of diseases will spread throughout the house and can cause problems in succeeding seasons. Pests will lay eggs which can overwinter in the house, resisting low temperatures without any difficulty. These hatch the following year to cause further attacks. The glass house red spider mite is a typical example of such a pest which can become established in crevices in houses and be a source of re-invasion in succeeding seasons.

Detailed instructions on coping with pests and diseases are given in the next chapter.

Pests and Diseases

A full list of every possible hazard that precious plants might have to endure, would so alarm a prospective greenhouse owner as to suggest that it would be more sensible to spend the money instead on a beach hut and worry about nothing but the incoming tide. This is an unnecessarily gloomy view. The positive approach, as advised in the previous chapter, is to take every possible precaution to prevent disaster, but if it does happen, deal with it promptly, because when something goes wrong in a greenhouse, it goes wrong at speed.

Precautions

Pots and boxes must be scrubbed before they are used; staging kept clean; no dead leaves or rubbish left on the floor as an inviting 'feather bed' to breed pests and diseases. Tools must be cleaned regularly.

Plants raised for outdoor planting give few problems if the hygiene is strict and the watering and ventilation correct. They should start outdoor life fit for anything, without having had any chemical treatment. Plants which are raised under glass, to remain there, need a more careful eye kept on them, so that at the first sign of anything unusual on, or with a plant, you can take immediate action.

Root troubles in the greenhouse, as we have seen, are usually caused by impure composts and unsterilized soil. It is false economy to take a chance. Use fresh compost and mixes and get the added benefit of freedom from weeds which compete with your plants and might even bring in their own problems of pests and diseases which can then spread quickly through the house. Always feed, ventilate and water carefully and you will not often have to consult those alarming illustrated charts of diseased, collapsed and bug-ridden plants suggesting what might have gone wrong.

Basic cleaning

The inside of the greenhouse should be cleaned thoroughly at least once a year. Use a disinfectant or detergent solution, and starting on the roof, with a long-handled broom, wash the glass and glazing bars, using a knife bent at the handle, or thin strip of plastic to get between the overlapping panes; these are likely 'hides' for pests and diseases (see drawing 92). Scrub the staging, woodwork, walls (see below) and floor, again using a disinfectant solution, and finally hose down the entire inside with clear water. Then hose down the outside glass too (see drawing 93). Never leave thinnings, tomato sideshoots, dead plants or leaves on the floor of the greenhouse. Tip old soil or compost out of pots or containers and scrub them thoroughly before storing.

Concrete or brick walls These are also lairs for pests and must be scrubbed and disinfected at least once a year. When dry, apply a freshly mixed lime wash to destroy fungus spores and pests; this will also add more light to the house.

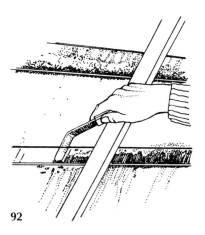

92

93

The best time to do these jobs is in winter when there are usually fewer plants in the house to be moved out of the way.

Dealing with trouble

Keep a most watchful eye on the plants and take prompt action when you see something you hoped not to. Modern chemicals take care of most troubles likely to appear, by sprays, aerosol dispenser, puffer packs, or watered with a systemic insecticide. But there are risks in using them in small houses filled with a variety of plants some of which may be oversensitive to particular sprays which are intended for their neighbours but drift their way. Also crops which are treated with some insecticides cannot be eaten for some time afterwards, so that in a small, assorted house, other crops nearly ripe will be useless, or at least risky. The safest to use among mixed crops, to which no plant is over-sensitive, is derris. Should indoor trouble get out of hand, in spite of all your precautions, you may find fumigation the simplest cure.

Fumigating a greenhouse

Use a special Aerosol or a smoke dispenser. Calculate the volume to be treated. Keep strictly to the instructions on the product, particularly about the age and type of plants in the house. A still warm evening is the best time . . . not during sunny weather.

Before starting, block any known cracks and close the house down. Treat each smoke bomb according to instructions, usually placing it on a sheet of glass or other non-inflammable material. Light according to instructions, starting at the end furthest from the exit of the house. *Proceed quickly, avoiding breathing in the smoke as far as possible and leaving the house as soon as all the smoke bombs have ignited.* If the house is not to be entered for a few hours after treatment, *lock the door,* particularly if there is any chance of a child or old person wandering in, and put a 'Keep Out' notice on it. If any of the smoke bombs does not ignite quite properly, *do not attempt to go back into the house* but leave until morning and repeat the treatment the next evening with a fresh 'smoke'. In the morning after treatment open up the house and let in as much air as the weather permits to ventilate the house thoroughly before going back inside to work.

Pests
Below is a short list of the most likely enemies of your greenhouse growing plans and how to cope with them.

Aphids
The name covers a range of insects including blackfly and greenfly. These tiny lice-like horrors suck the sap of young shoots, and undersides of young leaves. Their miniature Dracula existence weakens the plant so that leaves fall off and the new growth is distorted.

Remedy Use liquid derris, Topgard dust, malathion, or one of the systemic products like dimethoate. Gamma HCH smokes are also effective.

Mealy Bug
Related to the aphids, it is covered in a wool-like, white, waxy secretion which protects it against water. Masses form on stems or leaves, choosing vines, peaches, nectarines and general greenhouse pot plants.

Remedy During growing season, spray with systemic insecticide like dimethoate or malathion and repeat 14 days later. Spray vines before the berries swell.

Red Spider
Tiny mites, not true spiders but yet another family of sap-suckers. They get together on the underside of leaves, which then become discoloured and drop off (*see drawing 94*).

Remedy. Increase the humidity if this will not upset other inhabitants, and use sprays and dusts based on malathion and derris.

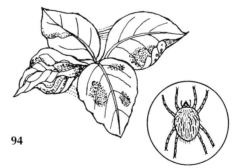

94

Vine weevil
The grubs feed on the roots not only of the vine, but pot plants such as cyclamen and tuberous begonias. They also attack the leaves and cause wilting.

Remedy Drench at first sign of attack with Gamma HCH.

Whitefly

These tiny winged moth-like insects have a particular appetite for tomatoes and cucumbers under glass. They then lay eggs on the leaves which become coated in a sticky film as the larvae suck the life out of the plant (*see drawing 95*).

Remedy Fumigate with DDT; use a malathion Aerosol or liquid spray. Follow instructions about repeated applications.

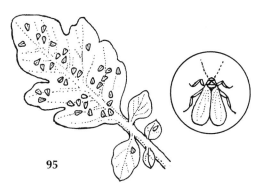

95

Diseases

Botrytis (Grey mould)

A fungus described by its name and far too often seen, usually where there is not enough ventilation. Plants such as lettuce rot and keel over at soil level; the disease is encouraged by dead plant material lying about, so hygiene is important.

Remedy Spray base of seedlings and plants with systemic fungicide such as benomyl. Because of the risk that resistant strains of the fungus can appear if they are not already present, alternate the use of benomyl with other substances such as dichlofluanid.

Brown root rot

A complex of diseases attacking tomato root systems, sometimes called 'corky root' from the brown, corklike appearance of the roots. Increases with each year that tomatoes are grown in the floor of the house causing stunted growth and reduced cropping although the flavour of the fruit in affected plants is usually excellent (*see drawing 96*).

96

Remedy After about three crops in the same soil, preventative measures have to be taken such as re-soiling, growing in containers of sterilized soil or compost, in peat growing bags or ring culture. Treatment with fungicides is not very effective. Commercial producers partially sterilize the soil between each crop using chemical or steam.

Damping off

A sadly common happening, particularly with learner greenhouse owners. It is a fungus disease which, under glass, attacks seedlings just above soil level, and describes their collapse and sudden death. It can be

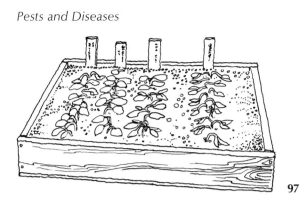

97

caused by seed sown too thickly, and without enough ventilation. The disease usually originates from general lack of hygiene or unsterilized soil or compost. This must be discarded or sterilized (*see drawing 97*).

Remedy Water seedlings with Captan or Cheshunt Compound.

Powdery mildew

A fungal disease which attacks many crops, but especially marrows, cucumbers and grapes. The leaves are covered with a white fungus, and the fruits rot.

Remedy Spray with systemic fungicide such as benomyl at first sign of attack and repeat every two weeks; or use dinocap.

Warning Never be clever when using chemicals, or think you know it all without reading the instructions carefully. Manufacturers have spent millions of pounds and around ten years testing each product before it is allowed to reach the amateur home grower. Do as you are told!

Follow these simple rules for safety's sake – *you* may know exactly what's what, but others may not.

1 Keep all gardening products, including disinfectants, locked away or on a high shelf where children, elderly people whose sight may be failing, and pets cannot reach them.

2 Never keep a left-over solution of a chemical but get rid of it.

3 Never, ever decant a chemical, or solution of a chemical, into a bottle which could be mistaken by someone else for a drink.

4 Don't keep anything that's lost its label and which may not be identifiable by someone else.

5 Do not smoke while using a chemical.

6 Wash any skin area that has come into contact with a chemical.

Month by Month

January

Sow seeds of tomato and cucumber, if the greenhouse has sufficient heat. Strawberries in pots, taken as baby runners from the outdoor parent plant can be brought indoors for fruiting in April to May. Lettuce, cauliflower, cabbage, broccoli, Brussels sprouts, can all be sown in the heated greenhouse at around 7–8°C (45°F).

January to February seeds should be ready to plant out in April; February to March seeds, in May. Set out potatoes to sprout in trays if the greenhouse is not going to admit any frost. The vine should have been pruned in autumn, but there is still time early in the month if you overlooked this. Keep bringing in roots of rhubarb, chicory and seakale for forcing, so you have a continuous supply rather than a glut.

February

Sow leeks, onions, early round-seeded peas, radish and sprouts and cauliflower if those sown the month before are not emerging to your liking. Prick out any seedlings big enough to pick up by one leaf, into potting compost. Bear in mind that ventilation is tricky at this time, with spasmodic bursts of sun and cold winds.

Plant some potatoes in 25 cm (10 in) pots to grow inside for some extra early 'new' ones – or if you can spare the space, put them in the border soil of the greenhouse. The crop will be small but delicious.

March

Sow melons, sweet peppers, aubergines (egg plant) French beans, tomatoes, celery, cress, mustard, more lettuce, cabbage, and cauliflower and any sowings which were forgotten in the last two months. Check potatoes set to sprout for outdoor planting. If there is any sign of an aphis attack, dust with derris. Rub out some of the shoots of a grapevine as they appear, leaving only one fruiting shoot every 45 cm (18 in) or so. By the end of the month it should be safe to sow tomatoes in an unheated house. Keep a watchful eye on ventilation in changeable spring weather, and don't allow tender seedlings to be baked near the glass in hot sunshine.

April

Sowing listed for the earlier months can still be made as well as second sowings, including melons. Sow runner beans for planting out later, sweet pepper, ridge cucumbers for growing outside, marrow (courgettes) and tomatoes for later planting in the open. Early tomatoes grown in a heated house must be fed from the time the first fruit trusses have fruit on them the size of a pea. Remove side shoots as they form. It is usually safe to plant tomatoes in unheated houses from the middle of the month. If in the border however at soil temperatures below about 14°C (57°F) little root growth takes place and plants grow better in containers on the surface of the soil.

Keep the vine under control by continually rubbing out surplus shoots as they appear.

May

Hardening off time and planting out. Critical for food crops. Choosing the wrong moment can undo all the benefit you have gained from a greenhouse. Everything depends on the weather and your own judgment. By the end of the month there should be little danger of frosts, but it is useless to put out half-hardy plants until the soil is warm. Seedlings raised indoors must have uninterrupted growth and may not recover from a set back in time to give a good crop. Put celery outside to harden off, also tomatoes for fruiting outside. Plant sweet pepper (capsicum) seedlings in the greenhouse border or into larger pots of growing compost. Any which are to be put out under cloches to fruit must be hardened off, so there is no check in their growth. Make repeat sowings of lettuce and other quick-growing crops for which there is a continuous demand, so there is no gap. Keep melons and cucumbers trained to their wires, and put a top dressing of compost when their roots appear above the surface of the soil. Strawberries which have finished fruiting indoors may be planted outside to recover and make runners.

June

The spring rush is over, and now it is mostly caretaker work. The temperature under glass can fluctuate wildly in sun, rain or cloud. To keep the greenhouse on an even keel, have plenty of ventilation when it is sunny, and shade if necessary, with a variety of preparations on sale to paint on the glass, or use lime wash, or special 'sunshade' materials. Warmth inevitably brings pests. Take action as soon as you spot any activity.

Remove male cucumber flowers before they open, to avoid pollination of female flowers which results in bitter fruit. Melons, though, should be hand-pollinated when several female flowers develop together. This helps to avoid uneven development of the fruits. Restrict each melon plant to 5–6 female flowers; they cannot take the strain of more.

Remove lateral shoots from tomatoes, and keep them trained and securely tied in. Tomatoes are required to make fresh growth and swell the fruit they are already carrying. Give feeds high in nitrogen possibly at every watering. Beware of rampant growth in the grapevine. Nip out any shoots which have started new growth after they have been stopped beyond the bunch of fruit.

July

Keep making small sowings of mustard, cress, lettuce, radish and annual tender herbs. Melons need to lap up sunshine for the fruits to ripen properly. Take off any leaves which are shading the maturing fruit, and go easy with the water. Support the fruit in nets. Stop tomatoes. Thin aubergines to 3–4 fruits a plant. Thin grape bunches if necessary, using sharp pointed scissors. Each bunch consists of several tiny bunches. Snip one or two grapes off each of these.

The main problem this month is ventilation and watering. Plants may have to be watered more than once a day, and on really hot days, as well as maximum ventilation, the floor should be dampened. Sprays are sure to be necessary for controlling pests and diseases, but wait until the bees and other harmless insects have retired for the night.

August

Cucumbers will start to slow down their growth, but will still need top dressings of compost or soil. Harvest the fruit continuously for they should be eaten when young and the more you eat the more the plant will obligingly provide.

Tomato plants must be stopped when the growing point reaches the roof, if this has not already been done. They will be producing ripe fruit and probably a forest of leaves which can prevent air from circulating freely through the plants. To reduce the risk of leaf mould and other fungus attacks, take off some of the leaves, sparingly. Snap off some of the lower leaves especially if they are yellow. The object is to let in air, not sun. The fruit does not need direct sun to ripen and, in fact it can cause 'greenback'. With a heavy load of fruit, tomato plants continue to need an extra dressing of nitrogen now as well as their regular feeding.

September

Ease off the regular feeding of plants. As days shorten and overnight temperatures fall, do as much watering as possible in the morning to reduce night time humidity, and the risk of botrytis. The earlier in the evening ventilation is reduced, the more heat will stay inside, but don't shut everything up in a hurry or this will increase the condensation problem. Cut down on the watering and keep a happy medium with plants neither too wet nor dried out. As their growth slows down they need less.

Remove yellowed leaves from cucumbers, tomatoes, melons and any other indoor plants, as they are doing no good and can breed infection. Clear the tomato crop if space is wanted for other plants and ripen the remaining fruit by hanging the whole plants or individual trusses from the roof.

Remove any shading from the glass, so the sun can have a last fling, and if possible give the glass a good clean at the same time to get maximum benefit.

October

Sow lettuce seed in boxes, and bring in the first chicory roots for forcing. Harvest the tomato crop and burn all old plants. Be ruthless about throwing out plants which are exhausted, though still bearing embryo fruit. They have served you well all season. Better pull them up rather than keep them for the sake of ripening one more melon, cucumber or tomato truss. A declining plant is much more prone to pests and disease than one in full vigour. Have a good tidy up and keep the house well ventilated so that the air is dry. Dampness through condensation is the danger this month.

November

Bring in seakale roots for forcing, and plant strips of mint roots in boxes of soil to force for use in winter when the outdoor plants shed their leaves. Take great care watering lettuce sown last month, to avoid wetting the leaves. Any seedling showing signs of mould must be removed instantly. Sow some more seeds for succession, of a different variety, to make a change.

This is the great clean-up time to ensure you start the coming new year with a spick, span and healthy growing house. Put outside everything which can stand the winter and scrub them clean – pots, boxes, all containers, bamboo canes, labels, watering cans – anything which could possibly harbour pests or disease. Some items can go back inside later when you have dealt with their purification.

Clean the house all over with a stiff brush dipped in disinfectant, using as little water as possible. Then treat the interior of a wooden house, making sure there are no nooks and crannies where insect eggs may be deposited; lime wash is satisfactory for this. Any rust should be treated first with a special metal paint. All this fuss is not for decoration. The purpose is to preserve the structure of the house, and purify it for the inhabitants. The outside work can be done whenever the weather allows it. Give priority to the inside cleaning during any slack period, which will depend on what you are growing or forcing. During the hubbub take a minute or two to sow a few lettuce and herb seeds.

Hygiene is also dealt with in *Routine Care* and *Pests and Diseases*.

December Bring in some rhubarb for forcing. This should have been lifted from the garden earlier and left out exposed to the frost, to produce delicious blanched shoots within about 6 weeks when forced under the greenhouse staging. Bring in a few roots at a time so you can enjoy the crop over a long period. Once the leaves have fallen from the grapevine, it should be dormant, and you can prune it and also rub off the loose bark. Should there have been any mildew during the growing period, paint the rods (stems) of the vine with a paste made up of Bordeaux powder and water.

This is a quiet time for greenhouse propagation and growing and gives a good breathing space to study catalogues and plan the coming year's programme.

Keeping a record

Make a New Year resolution to keep a large diary or record book and promise yourself to fill in a weekly account of what you and your plants have been doing, in and out of the greenhouse. It is the only way you will ever learn from mistakes; find the right timings for your particular greenhouse and part of the country; remember which varieties you liked best and those which, for your needs and conditions, were a waste of space and time. I use black and green pens, and mark failures and successes with as many black crosses or green ticks as I think they deserve. It makes decisions for the following year much less of an agony.

Part 3

Choosing, Installing and Equipping Your Greenhouse

Plan for the future when choosing your greenhouse and try to avoid 'thinking small'. Obviously the space available in your garden and indeed how much you can afford to spend must have a bearing on the size of greenhouse you will choose but a sound maxim is to buy the largest you can afford. Remember that, apart from the benefits of extra working space, the larger the volume of air, the less extreme is the heating and cooling, small greenhouses suffering particularly from extremes of heat and cold as well as problems with draught-free ventilation. If, for practical reasons you can only start with a small greenhouse, make it if possible 2.45 m (8 ft) wide, and give consideration to a make that allows extension at a later date. This will enable you, once you have gained some experience, to increase the range of crops grown.

A cheap popular greenhouse will serve a purpose, but the more expensive structures are more strongly built and often have refinements in the matter of glazing. Some of the best are scaled-down versions of commercial houses. Some 'expensive' greenhouses come with a great deal of equipment in them, but I would recommend the best structure you can afford and then add equipment later on. You can always add equipment, but you cannot change the basic greenhouse structure once you have bought it. Departmental stores are a good source for the mass-produced models and offer extremely good value. Garden centres or purchase direct from the factory are better for models with more refinements and where design characteristics are important.

The wooden frame
You will have a choice of wood or aluminium framework. These days, there is little difference in price. Wood is a poor conductor of heat compared with aluminium, so a wooden greenhouse is slightly warmer. It is true to say that it blends better with the natural surroundings and, if cedar is chosen rather than white softwood, maintenance can be confined to treating with a red cedar liquid preservative every few years. It is probably better than aluminium in coastal areas where the salt in the air will attack aluminium and cause a rather unsightly white powder corrosion. Wood also resists sulphur fumes in industrial areas, but on the debit side, it is inclined to discolour badly where there are soot deposits.

A wooden greenhouse allows you to put up shelves and accessories just where you want them, using simple wood screws and it also eliminates condensation on the glazing bars. If it is delivered ready glazed in six pieces as is sometimes the case, this saves a great deal of work; otherwise glazing is a rather messy business involving a bedding on either putty or mastic and sprigs (headless tacks). The glazing bars are wider than on comparable sized aluminium houses, so a little more light is excluded.

Painting a greenhouse is not really advisable although it does look attractive; the high humidity often results in peeling paint and maintenance becomes a regular and very tedious chore. Even if the greenhouse is made of softwood, it is better to use a modern liquid

A *Electric switch panel;* B *Staging;* C *Paraffin heater;* D *Electric fan heater;* E *Tubular heaters;* F *Capillary bench;* G *Roof ventilators (automatically controlled);* H *Extractor fan;* I *Mist unit and heated bed (controlled by thermostat);* J *Fluorescent lights;* K *Propagator with plastic cover (automatically heated);* L *Pesticide vaporiser;* M *Wall ventilator;* N *Rod thermostat (controls tubular heaters);* O *Slatted blind (external);* P *Roller blind (internal);* Q *Maximum and minimum thermometer;* R *Shelving for plants;* S *Trickle watering system.*

preservative. Red cedar preservative can be used to increase the life of whitewood. This treatment looks well and lasts well.

Even if a wooden greenhouse is not supplied pre-glazed, the fitting of the six assemblies is simple and quick. The framework is strong and firm enough to be rigid, even before the glass is fitted. The resultant finished greenhouse is therefore heavier than an aluminium house and also very stable. On the face of it, the expected life should be shorter with a wooden greenhouse, but regularly treated with preservative this does not need to be the case.

Most wooden framed greenhouses are glazed with glass, but for positions where glass might be broken there are wooden greenhouses glazed with clear ICI Novolux plastic sheeting which is guaranteed against deterioration for five years. Wooden framing is also being used for some of the more recently introduced plastic greenhouses.

The aluminium frame

Aluminium has become the most widely used material for greenhouse framing. It has many advantages. It is maintenance free, and even if impurities in the air cause it to oxidise, the coating of white powder does no harm. Indeed it can prevent further deterioration. It is comparatively light, which means that the greenhouse framework can be assembled on any flat surface, such as a lawn, and then carried over to the foundations for glazing. The aluminium extrusions lend themselves to packaging in kit form, which simplifies and reduces the cost of delivery, but it increases the erection time – indeed simplicity of erection is very much dependent upon the manufacturer and the quality of his instructions. Sometimes every part is coded: more frequently there are separate parcels for each section of the greenhouse.

Practically all the aluminium extrusions are slotted in the inner surface. This is done for assembly reasons, the bolts being captive in the slots and the nuts being placed on the bolts from inside the greenhouse, but these same slots are also used, in conjunction with cropped bolts, for the fitting of accessories such as shelves, water tanks and ventilator openers.

Metal, unlike wood, being a good conductor of heat, aluminium glazing bars transmit heat readily to the outside, and the 'fins' which most glazing bars form, are added coolers, especially in windy conditions. This is demonstrated by the amount of condensation so often seen on the inside of aluminium glazing bars, but remember that, compared with the glass area, the losses through the metal are comparatively small. As a compensating factor aluminium greenhouses transmit more light than wooden ones.

Provided one is prepared to pay for it, the problem of aluminium discoloration can be overcome by purchasing a greenhouse which has an epoxy-coated frame. They are available in both green and white and, in the right surroundings, look very attractive.

The method of glazing aluminium structures varies according to the make. Generally, 60 cm (2 ft) square glass panes are used because this is a standard easily obtainable size, it is not too expensive to renew and, above all, it can be transported easily. The panes are usually secured with clips which may be of aluminium or of stainless steel. Some more expensive greenhouses have smooth plates screwed to the structure to clamp the glass in position; this system is much superior to clips as it puts an even pressure on the glass, reduces dirt traps in the glazing bars and eliminates cooling due to 'fins' on the outer surface of the conventional glazing bar. The system also makes washing the exterior of the greenhouse much easier as it produces a relatively smooth surface. Whatever system is used to secure the glass, most greenhouses have the glass bedded on PVC strip although mastic is used occasionally. The former is easier to use, the latter when perfectly done, is watertight and draughtproof.

With 60 cm (2 ft) square panes, the necessary overlapping creates dirt and algae traps at the overlap, which also makes it difficult to obtain a complete windproof seal at the point of maximum overlap. For this reason some manufacturers use 1·20 m (4 ft) or 1·40 m (4 ft 6 in) panes and overlap is not then needed. The panes can be bedded directly on to the aluminium glazing bars without the need for mastic or PVC tubing. Such large panes may be expensive to renew, but they do not become dirt traps, the light transmission is good and they look attractive. In areas of high winds there is a tendency for rain to be driven upwards into the greenhouse where glass overlaps.

'Plastic' versus glass
Although the conventional greenhouse is glazed with glass, the use of polythene or PVC in place of glass is increasing and has certainly made the acquisition of a greenhouse possible for those who could not afford a glass house. Even so, there is no doubt that glass is a better proposition

A simple, polythene-clad model

'Bubble film' used as a form of double glazing

for those that can afford it. Apart from low initial cost the only advantages of a plastic house are firstly the lightness of the structure, which allows it to be moved from one part of the garden to another without too much difficulty, so avoiding the need for soil sterilization, and secondly, its safety where children playing ball may break the glass.

The disadvantages are the fact that the outer skin discolours and usually needs renewing after on average about two years, the plastic radiates the heat from inside the greenhouse at night more than glass and it also poses major problems because of the difficulty of achieving good ventilation control. This is of particular importance if you are trying to grow lettuces very early in the year.

Most plastic greenhouses use a flexible 600 gauge film stretched over galvanised steel tubing, but recently attempts have been made to imitate the shape of traditional glass houses by using a wooden frame. Aluminium tubing is also employed. One particular design uses a traditional wooden frame glazed with rigid corrugated ICI Novolux plastic sheet which is guaranteed for five years: this is an excellent greenhouse for places where ball damage is very likely, but it costs nearly as much as a glass house, and, as with polythene sheeting, drips from condensation can be a problem.

Condensation is a major problem in all small plastic covered greenhouses both because the droplets reduce the light that passes through, and also because there is an increase in humidity and the constant moisture can lead to a growth of algae. The humidity may not matter in late spring and summer when plenty of ventilation is usually given anyway, but it can be fatal to winter crops, which become victims of fungus troubles.

Ventilation of a plastic greenhouse is usually simple to the point of being crude, by openings in the doors at the front and rear, but recent designs show that attempts are now being made to incorporate separate side or end ventilators, which may well improve their growing capabilities. The plastic cover or envelope is usually stretched over the frame in one piece and the surplus at the bottom buried well in the soil or held down by paving slabs to make the greenhouse windproof. If the cover is put on in warm weather a tighter job is made than if the polythene is put over in cold weather. This both looks better and is less likely to flap in the wind with greater risk of tearing.

Some plastic greenhouses are available with a double skin. This is fine for retaining the heat, but it aggravates still further the problem of light absorption just at the time of year that we want all the light we can get.

Some attractive shapes have been designed, but, by and large, a polythene clad greenhouse is not an attractive addition to the garden. Small polythene-clad lean-to greenhouses at a modest price have recently made their appearance and are suitable for tomato growing against walls.

Which to choose?
Even apart from cost considerations, making the choice from the enormous array of 'popular' greenhouses is extremely difficult. In the first

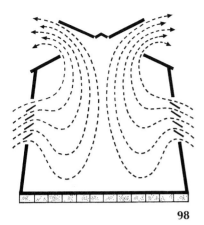

98

*Louvre ventilators assist
free movement of air*

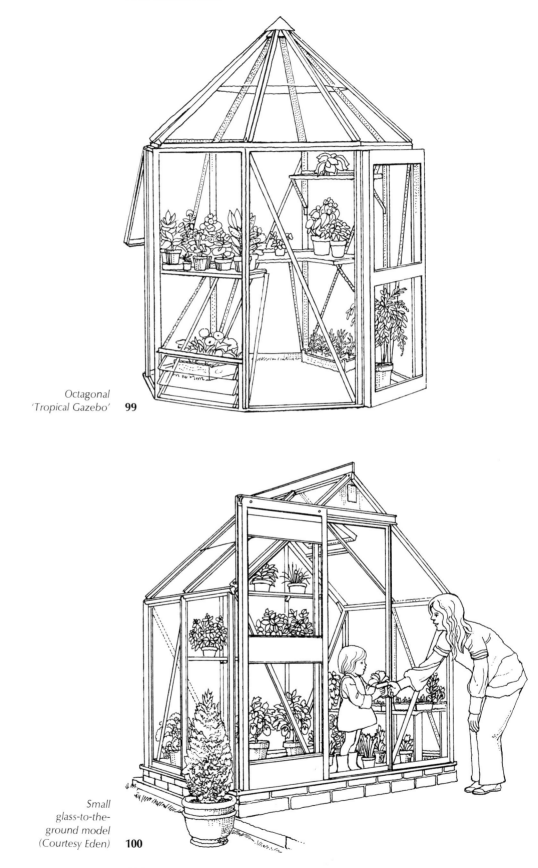

Octagonal 'Tropical Gazebo' **99**

Small glass-to-the-ground model (Courtesy Eden) **100**

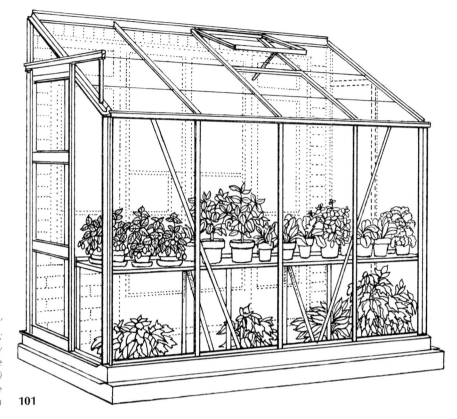

A typical 'walk in' lean-to (Hall's); ventilation is tricky though louvre ventilators (below) help solve the problem **101**

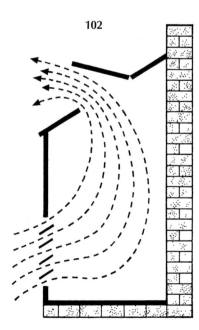

accessories like heaters and water tanks, although staging and shelving is well catered for. Rather more unusual than the multi-sided shape is a geodetically constructed round domed model, using triangular panes of glass. Light transmission is first class, but the staging is rather low.

A design feature one needs to consider when choosing a greenhouse is whether we are to have glass to the ground. With an aluminium house, there is no option, but if you are using staging it is a waste to allow heat to escape underneath, so some form of double glazing should be used (see below). With wooden greenhouses you can, in fact, buy them half-boarded all round or on one side only. Boarding on one side saves heat, provided you are certain that you are always going to use staging, but ground level salad crops are not going to be very happy without glass to the ground. The *vegetable* greenhouse is probably best with the glass to the ground all round (*see drawing 100*).

Lean-to greenhouses are available in wood and metal. They have the advantage that if they are built on to the dwelling house they are handy of access in bad weather, they are warm and services such as water, electricity and gas are easily conveyed (*see drawing 101*). The disadvantages are lack of light, excessive heat thrown back by the brick wall during the summer and ventilation problems (*see diagram 102*). With bungalows, the eaves allow insufficient fall for the roof to prevent condensation drip and rain blowing in: the only really satisfactory way to overcome this is to have a three-quarter span greenhouse – which also tends to alleviate the other problems of light, overheating and

Another type of lean-to (Marley); suitable when space is too restricted for a walk-in model **103**

ventilation, but it is a relatively expensive form of construction.

Lean-to's, like conventional greenhouses, can be custom built in either wood or aluminium; various different types and sizes are available (*see drawing 103*).

Another design feature to look for is eave height. The higher the eaves, the better the working height, especially when growing tomatoes or using shelves in addition to staging, but, of course, a high eaved greenhouse with vertical sides uses more material than a low eaved model of the same nominal size and is usually more expensive. Eave heights vary from 1·20 m (4 ft) to 1·75 m (5 ft 9 in). Unless the greenhouse is a very expensive model, high eaves mean a shallower roof angle, but to prevent condensation drip on to the plants, the angle should not be less than 20 deg. A shallow angle may also be a disadvantage where heavy snowfall can be expected.

Whatever the size of greenhouse chosen, give some thought to the doors. Generally speaking a sliding door is better than a hinged door: it is easier to open when you are carrying seed trays since you can slide it with your foot, and it is certainly much less likely to be damaged by wind. Most doors are only 60 cm (2 ft) wide: if you are growing crops that need soil sterilization or renewal, consider a make with a 1·20 m (4 ft) door, which is wide enough for a wheelbarrow or even an invalid chair.

Staging and shelving
Staging is most often sold as part of the greenhouse. If it is actually fixed to the structure it has the advantage of being perfectly level, which is

absolutely essential if you are using capillary watering. On the other hand, free-standing staging has the advantage of versatility so that you can place it either side or even at the end of the greenhouse. If you are going to do much serious propagating it must be really strong to carry the weight of the compost which can be very heavy. The staging can be all wood, although aluminium is more general today, sometimes with clear or composition slats. Slats are preferable to solid staging, especially for pot plants, because they allow air to circulate between the plants, but the slats should be movable so that they can be set together to form a flat surface for capillary watering (see page 124). Some aluminium slats are reversible to present a flat surface on one side and a tray about an inch deep on the other. Seedlings can be grown directly in the tray.

Plastic staging with built-in electric heating is also available. Some new aluminium staging has been designed to provide quick and easy dismantling and compact storage. Another specialist design has rollers instead of bars and each roller can be removed independently, an excellent idea when you need to maintain your propagating bench, but also want to make room for a few tall plants in the ground bed to come up through the staging.

Shelving is another useful addition to make the maximum use of your greenhouse. Made of aluminium it is mounted on brackets that are secured to the vertical glazing bars with cropped bolts inserted into the glazing bar slots.

Support systems and 'room dividers'

Various proprietary crop support systems are obtainable for plants such as tomatoes and melons. A typical example is an aluminium ring which attaches to a cropped bolt inserted in a glazing bar slot at the desired position. Twine or supporting cord can be tied to this and to a peg in the ground. There are variations on the idea, all designed to carry the plant up to the top of the roof. Ensure before using the framework of the house to support the crop that it is capable of taking the weight of plants in crop. If you are growing warmth-loving plants like melons and tomatoes and you are buying a fairly large greenhouse, you will not want to heat the whole greenhouse all the time, so consider a model which can be fitted with a divider unit to provide, in effect, a separate warm and a cool house. You can achieve the same objective more cheaply, but less effectively and conveniently, by hanging a sheet of 600 gauge polythene across the greenhouse to separate the two areas.

Choosing the site

The siting of a greenhouse is a real problem in an 'average' garden. Ideally, it should be in an open position so that it receives the sun all day. For the same reason a rectangular greenhouse should run from east to west. This ensures that the maximum use is made of the winter sunlight: if you mainly use your greenhouse in the spring and summer, its main axis should be north south so that plants receive equal amounts of light on both sides.

However, practicalities so often dictate that the greenhouse should be near the house. Certainly, human nature being what it is, a greenhouse is not likely to have all the attention it needs during the bad winter weather if it is down the bottom of the garden. In addition, the provision of a path and of electricity and water are likely to be both difficult and very expensive, so, on balance, most people will get the best overall results by placing the greenhouse in the lightest possible position within about 4·50 m (15 ft) of the house, or perhaps even nearer if the back of the house faces south. If you have large trees nearby work out their shadow pattern in winter and early spring and try to avoid it.

Very often it is convenient from an access point of view to place a greenhouse at the side of a house, but bear in mind this is always a draughty spot and heating costs will be increased. If you have a separate single-storey garage, behind this can often be an accessible and sheltered spot without losing too much light. If the greenhouse is slightly shaded, say by a fence, on one side, more than the other, you will sometimes find that by putting the staging on the shady side, the shade does no harm as the bench will be high enough off the ground not to be affected.

Erecting the greenhouse

Greenhouse erection starts with the foundations, and the entire success of the project depends upon this job being done correctly. A few years ago, few greenhouses were supplied with their own foundations and it was then necessary to make a foundation of brick or concrete. Today, many models have either asbestos strengthening panels built into the greenhouse or sectional foundations in wood, steel or aluminium can be purchased to fit the particular house.

Whatever system is used, the first thing to do is to find out from the makers the *exact* outer dimensions of the base. Nominal sizes just will not do. Then dig out roughly a trench about 15 cm (6 in) deep to these measurements. If you are using concrete or brick foundations, put in a base of hardcore and then build your brick or concrete wall so that the outer dimensions exactly tally with the greenhouse. In particular make sure that the foundations are *exactly* square. This is checked by taking the two diagonal measurements, which must be exactly equal. This diagonal measurement must be checked whatever kind of foundations you use and it must be accurate.

If you have a sloping garden and you have to cut into the ground at the upper end, you may have a hump of soil in the middle that prevents you making a direct diagonal measurement. One way of overcoming this problem is to make up accurately in wood a giant set square with arms about 1·80 m (6 ft) long. With this you can check each of your right angles instead of measuring the diagonals.

Building a pre-fabricated foundation
Dig out a trench about 15 cm (6 in) deep, and level it with aggregate or sand. Most prefabricated bases are fitted with bolt-on legs which have to be buried in concrete, so dig out the correct number of holes to the

required depth – usually about 50–60 cm (18–24 in). Make up the base on the lawn, bolting the sections together only loosely, and lift the base into position, having already attached the legs. Sit the legs, in the holes, making up with rammed aggregate so that the base is the correct height and all sections are level. Use a spirit level to check this. The base should now be quite firm and should be adjusted for squareness by a diagonal check. When this is correct tighten all the bolts and recheck that the base has not moved out of square during the tightening.

Now fill in the holes with cement so that the legs are well bedded in the centre. Recheck for squareness again before the concrete is hardened. After a couple of days to allow the concrete to harden, the assembled greenhouse can be bolted to the base. If a wooden base is used it must be well treated with preservative; better still, if the wood has been 'tanalised', *ie*, commercially treated so that it has been impregnated with preservative under pressure, before purchase.

This is the time to lay on water, gas or electricity services – which if left until later might necessitate some of your work being undone.

Assembling the sections

Greenhouse erection itself depends upon the type. Wooden green-houses may be supplied in six ready-glazed sections that only need bolting together, or, alternatively you may have to do the glazing yourself, by bedding the glass on putty or, better still, on to one of the modern non-hardening proprietary mastic compounds, finally securing with sprigs (headless tacks).

An aluminium greenhouse usually arrives in a bundle of dozens of parts. If you are good at jigsaws it will be easy to assemble, but makes do vary greatly in the difficulty of erection and the easiest to erect are not necessarily the best greenhouses. Sometimes the parts are in separate bundles, such as one each for the door, gable end, side and so on. If this is the case, the golden rule is: *never ever open any bundle until you are ready to assemble that particular section*. Other makers send the parts in one box with every part labelled and coded. Both systems have their devotees, but either way *do study the instruction booklet* for two or three evenings before you actually start work.

When you do start, assemble one section only at a time, starting at the gable end. Collect all the appropriate parts together, first in a bundle and then lay them out in the appropriate positions on the lawn. Bolt them together finger tight only and place the assembled frame safely out of the way. Note that some instructions call for bolts to be fed into the glazing bar channels for later use when fitting opening ventilators or accessories. If you omit to do this at the correct time you may have to do partial dismantling later. Do make sure you have help when joining up the sides together: if they are allowed to collapse the framework will be ruined. The job can be done without help if you use plenty of props both inside and outside the greenhouse.

When all six sides have been assembled and bolted together, still only finger tight, lift the whole assembly on to the foundations. Square the greenhouse base up very accurately with the foundations and then bolt it down. This is the time to tighten up *all* the greenhouse bolts with a spanner.

Glazing

You are now ready to start glazing. Sort the glass out so that you can glaze continuously in a methodical way, completing one side at a time, fitting the PVC strip or mastic first and then laying the glass on it. Usually it is best to start with the gable end, then the door end followed by the two sides and the roof.

A word of warning: accidents involving glass can be very nasty, especially when glazing the roof, so follow these simple safety rules.

1 Keep children and pets well clear of the area
2 Wear fairly thick gloves
3 Make sure the steps you are using are firm and safely positioned
4 Refrain from glazing on a windy day, especially if using large panes of glass
5 When glazing the roof a helper is an advantage, but don't let your assistant stand directly under the glass.

Make a point of following these precautions; I have known a complete pane to shatter merely through the noise caused by moving the glass along the aluminium glazing bar.

When using 60 cm (2 ft) square panes, start at the bottom and work upwards to ensure that the top glass always overlaps the lower glass so that the rain runs down the outside of the glass.

Although double-glazing is not something one would do at the same time as the initial glazing is done, it is something to consider if heat is to be conserved. The cheapest and easiest method is an internal lining of thin polythene, but it will cut down the light and introduce ventilation and condensation problems leading to high humidity and possibly disease. There are proprietary 60 cm (2 ft) square translucent plastic panels which can be clipped over the glass. These allow you to double-skin parts of the greenhouse only and do not affect ventilation. Wooden boarding can be used below the staging and a relatively new 'bubble' plastic sheeting, if carefully applied, will achieve excellent heat retention without interfering with ventilation or materially increasing condensation. Experiments have shown it to be remarkably effective although its life span may not exceed two seasons unless carefully preserved.

Accessories for your greenhouse

Greenhouse accessories are divided broadly into three categories – heating, watering and ventilation. Of these automatic ventilation is probably the most important and by no means the most expensive.

Ventilating

There are automatic ventilator openers which are operated by a plunger in conjunction with a cylinder containing a heat-sensitive expanding substance. The latest of these are very neat and can be quickly fitted to

Electric soil moisture indicator (Courtesy Diplex)

Automatic ventilator opener (Courtesy Baylis)

wooden greenhouses and the conventional aluminium greenhouse employing slotted glazing bars. Used in conjunction with low louvre ventilators, the greenhouse will take care of itself during the day. (See also *Routine Care*). More effective but more costly are electric extractor fans that fit into a pane of glass. They provide a positive air movement, calculated in cubic feet per minute, and are controlled by an independent rod type thermostat (again, see *Routine Care*).

A modestly priced simple oil greenhouse heater (Courtesy Aladdin)

Heating

A completely unheated greenhouse at the mercy of sudden sharp overnight frost, which can occur as late as May, is of only limited value and the addition of heating will make it considerably more useful. However, an unheated house is a start. Some form of heating, sufficient to keep it frost-free, transforms the greenhouse and makes it an all-the-year round asset but for some crops quite a considerable temperature 'lift' has to be provided if plant raising is going to be possible in the depths of winter.

Simple oil heaters are cheap to buy and have no installation costs. They can be fitted with pipes to distribute the hot air around the greenhouse. They also produce some carbon dioxide, which is good for plants in daylight conditions, and a great deal of water vapour, which in cold weather is a disadvantage. They also need wick trimming and oil filling every few days. Because they must be lit every night when there is any possibility of frost, they are not so cheap to operate as might be expected. Unfortunately, there are only two oil heaters which are thermostatically controlled and at the same time suitable for the amateur's relatively small greenhouse. Refined grades of paraffin only should be used in these heaters.

Natural gas is the cheapest form of fuel in cost per K/cal (BTU, British Thermal Unit) though partially offset by the need to provide ample ventilation and the losses due to the fact that the jet is always alight, whether it be a separate pilot jet or a main jet turned down low. Even allowing for this, it is likely to cost less than half that of electricity. It is thermostatically controlled, usually by a thermostat built in to the heater, but occasionally by a separate thermostat. It needs professional installation (or checking) for safety and produces both carbon dioxide and plenty of water, but no poisonous fumes in measurable quantity. Where natural gas is not available, bottled propane can be used and, although the running cost will then be comparable with electricity, it is a very suitable system for a greenhouse situated too far away from the house to warrant an electrical installation.

Heating by electricity

Without any doubt at all, electric heating is the cleanest and also the easiest and most accurate to control. It is also the most expensive to run except when the greenhouse is maintained at only 4·5°C (40°F), when the benefits will certainly outweigh any cost difference. At high temperatures such as 10°C (50°F) electricity is very expensive indeed. Remember that the cost of heating roughly doubles with each 3°C (5°F) that the thermostat setting is raised. Electricity could be used with an oil heater, set to come on only when the oil heater was not lit, or not adequate to deal with low temperatures, and the temperature fell dangerously low. The electrical installation is relatively expensive and for safety's sake should be approved by the Electricity Board, but without it, you not only lose out on electric heating but also on propagators, fans, and lighting too. Special greenhouse power distribution boards should always be used as domestic switchgear is quite unsuitable for the damp conditions found in the greenhouse.

There are broadly two types of electric heater available: the static tubular heater and the blower heater. Blowers, or *fan heaters* as they are known (*see drawing 104*) are usually free-standing on the floor of the greenhouse and are generally positioned about 30 cm (1 ft) from the end pointing down the path so that the hot air does not scorch the plants. The fan draws in cool air over a variable thermostat that monitors the temperature and forces it out again over the heating element. The fan keeps the air moving and maintains a buoyant atmosphere so reducing the conditions predisposing to fungal diseases. For this reason of air movement, most heaters have switches that allow the fan to run without the heating element. The fan can also be used to keep the air moving in very hot weather. The thermostat is built in to the fan heater and there

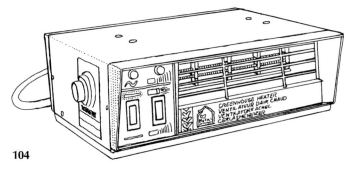

Fan heater designed for greenhouse use (Courtesy Humex) **104**

are no installation problems as the fan heater is plugged into the switch board. Good quality long-lasting models are by no means cheap and may well cost more than a fixed tubular heater system, although to the latter must be added the cost of a separate rod thermostat.

Tubular heaters, usually of non-rusting aluminium, are generally rated at 60 watts per 30 cm (1 ft) run and then made up to whatever wattage is needed to heat the greenhouse. Ideally the tubes should be installed along three sides of the greenhouse to achieve good heat distribution, any extra wattage required being achieved by double or triple banking. The thermostat controlling the heaters should be shielded from the morning sun to prevent false readings causing overcooling in shady parts of the greenhouse.

A formula which allows you to work out the size of heater you require in relation to the glass area of the greenhouse has been devised by the Electricity Council. The same formula can be used for gas and paraffin heaters which generally have an 'equivalent KW' rating. The procedure is as follows:

1 Measure the area of the glass and glazing bars in sq ft = (**a**)
2 Multiply (**a**) by 0·39 = (**b**)
3 Multiply (**b**) by the temperature 'lift' you require over outside temperature in degrees Fahrenheit. The base temperature can be taken as 32°F for heating from early March on (lower for an earlier start) and the top temperature from the cropping instructions for the most heat demanding crop you intend to grow.

The answer is in watts: choose the next largest standard size of heater. For practical purposes you can ignore the losses through the soil. Wooden sides should be multiplied by 0·5 and added to the glass area.

A reliable maximum/minimum thermometer should be fitted in the greenhouse so that the operation of the heating thermostat can be

Typical high-topped automatic electric propagator (Courtesy Humex)

*Another type
of propagator
(Courtesy Camplex)*

checked and also to allow you to measure the temperature variations throughout the greenhouse.

One way of keeping the overall temperature setting down in greenhouses is to use two of the electrically-heated and thermostatically controlled propagating frames; if chosen with sufficient head room – say 30 cm (1 ft) or more – they allow seeds and cuttings started off in a warm propagator to be hardened off in another propagator before transferring them to a greenhouse which is, perhaps, kept at only 4·5°C (40°F). During the winter the two propagators can be used to over-winter cold-sensitive plants such as runner bean roots. See also *Routine Care*.

Watering

This is a problem when you go on holiday, but watering can easily be automated, especially in the summer when a little over-watering does little harm. There are excellent automatic overhead sprays, but the wetting of the foliage can present problems and other forms are preferred. *Capillary watering* is the simplest. By this method plants in pots are stood on a synthetic water conducting material which dips at one end into a reservoir of water, which can either be hand filled, fed from an inverted bottle on the 'glug' system, or replenished automatically from the mains (using the garden hose and a water stop connector) through a ball-valve controlled tank. An adjustable fluid level controller on the bench prevents overflow. The controller is set by experiment to control the degree of saturation of the capillary matting. A similar system can be used in conjunction with gravel trays and sand beds, but these are very heavy.

In another form of automatic watering, the pots or boxes are watered from a *trickle line* with adjustable nozzles either spaced about 30 cm (1 ft) apart or one to each pot. The line is connected to a tank of water which

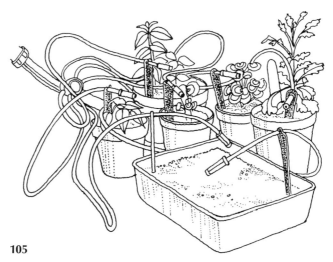

105

flushes automatically at intervals that vary according to the rate at which the tank is filled, which is usually a few drops a minute, from a large tank or the mains (*see drawing 105*). There is also a fine spray system that can be laid along a row of seed boxes, the spray nozzle being about 30 cm (1 ft) above them. The spray line is fed from the mains either hand-controlled or automatically through a monitor, such as an electric 'leaf' that operates an electro-magnetic water valve when it becomes dry. The same principle is used for mist propagation units but these are not likely to be required for vegetable growing.

Which to invest in first?

There is so much greenhouse equipment available that it is difficult to be categorical about priorities, but for the grower who is out all day I am sure that ventilation is the most important followed by automatic watering to take care of weekend breaks and holidays. Beyond this it is largely a matter of personal preference and individual circumstances. Even so, overriding even these considerations is some form of heating, be it only a simple oil heater. Without a means of keeping out severe late frosts you can never make your greenhouse a really economical proposition.

Index